ART

TREASURES

OF

THE

UFFIZI

AND

PITTI

TEXT BY

FILIPPO ROSSI

HARRY N. ABRAMS, INC.

NEW YORK

MILTON S. FOX, EDITOR

DESIGNED BY MARSHALL LEE

LIST OF PLATES

Arranged alphabetically by artist. All references are to plate numbers.

Color plates are indicated by italic type.

ART TREASURES OF THE UFFIZI & PITTI

THE UFFIZI & PITTI

Love of art was a tradition in the Medici family, rulers of Florence in the fifteenth century and princes of the State of Tuscany from 1530 onward. To this tradition belongs the origin of the collections which have made the two Florentine galleries, the Uffizi and the Pitti, famous all over the world. Today very little remains of what belonged to the Medici collections in the fourteen-hundreds. But these paintings and a few pieces of sculpture are enough to indicate the breadth of interest that distinguished the various members of the family. Not only did they aim to acquire the finest ancient statues that came from the soil of Rome, through the constant research of the Humanists; not only did they commission the best Florentine artists of the *quattrocento* for their own homes and villas, or even for the churches they

11

protected; but, with the comprehension and taste of true collectors, they also collected the works of foreign artists.

In the Medici palace on the Via Larga it was principally Cosimo the Elder and Lorenzo the Magnificent who had assembled the art treasures which are listed only in part in the inventory made in 1492 at Lorenzo's death. But, owing to the brevity of the descriptions, only few of the objects listed can be identified with those now in our Gallery. Through various documents we know that a few pieces of Classical sculpture now in the Gallery once belonged to the Medici collections. They include the so-called *Scipio* (today thought rather to represent a priest of Isis, because of its peculiar headdress), the bust of Marcus Agrippa, and the two statues of Marsyas tied to the tree and awaiting the punishment decreed for him by Apollo, whom he had imprudently defied. These statues are said to have been restored by Donatello and Verrocchio, but this is not absolutely certain.

Fortunately we have more information about the early Medici paintings: the *Entombment* by Rogier van der Weyden is most probably the altarpiece listed in the inventory as belonging to the chapel of the Villa Medici at Careggi near Florence; the triptych with the *Raising of Lazarus* by Nicholas Froment was probably sent by an agent of the Banco Mediceo to Cosimo the Elder, who gave it to the Convent of Bosco ai Frati in Mugello. Paolo Uccello painted the *Battle of San Romano* for the Medici family, and the inventory mentions that it was hung in the bedroom of the palace along with the other two panels of the *Battle* now in the Louvre and the National Gallery in London. For the chapel of the Medici villa at Cafaggiolo, where the family had its origin, Alesso Baldovinetti painted the altarpiece of the *Madonna and Child with Saints,* exhibited at the Uffizi since 1796. Also in Lorenzo's bedroom, along with Uccello's *Battle,* was a portrait of Galeazzo Maria Sforza by Piero del Pollaiuolo, which may have been painted when the Duke of Milan was a guest of the Magnificent in 1471; in Piero's bedroom a painting is described which is almost certainly Botticelli's *Pallas and the Centaur,* executed for Lorenzo or Giuliano de' Medici. There are several other paintings by Botticelli known to have been in the early Medici collection, such as the youthful *Portrait of a Man,* who holds a medal reproducing the features of Cosimo the Elder; and his two most famous compositions, the *Primavera* and the *Birth of Venus,* painted for Lorenzo di Pierfrancesco's villa of Castello near Florence. Luca Signorelli painted the Madonna with various figures in the background for Lorenzo the Magnificent.

The many treasures the Medici had collected in their Florentine palace and in their villas were often plundered and dispersed; first after their banishment from the city in 1494, later when they were exiled again in 1527, and a third time on the death of Alessandro, the first Medici duke. Cosimo I, Duke of the Florentine republic and later Grand Duke of Tuscany, was able to recover only a small part of the family's original collection. He established himself in the Palazzo Vecchio and had it enlarged and decorated by contemporary artists. Wishing to continue the family tradition, he formed a rare collection of works of art, which constituted the famous Medici *guardaroba* or "wardrobe," described in an inventory of 1553, and the goal of all visitors to the palace. The construction of the Uffizi Palace by Vasari offered the possibility of having an authentic gallery. It was enriched by a large loggia which seemed indeed a proper place to exhibit at least some of the ancient and contemporary statues owned by the Medici, then scattered in their many buildings and gardens.

This project was taken over by the successor of Cosimo I, Francesco, after the death of his father in 1574. The first loggia, on the eastern side, was adorned with grotesques by Giovanni Maria Butteri, Giovanni Bizzelli, and Alessandro Pieroni, and it housed, toward the end of the century, numerous sculptures which gave the gallery the original name of Gallery of the Statues. Of these

A GALLERY IN THE PITTI

it is also difficult to state exactly which and how many can be identified with the ones now exhibited in the Uffizi, since little information is given by the inventories and guides of that time. We know, however, from Francesco Bocchi and his *Bellezze di Firenze* (Beauties of Florence), published in 1591, that there were then about eighty statues in marble and bronze, and various busts. From the subsequent inventories we learn that the number of statues, busts, and ancient inscriptions was being rapidly augmented, due to the frequent purchases made in Rome by the agents of the Grand Duke, of which we have testimony in letters still preserved in the state archives in Florence. Portraits of famous men, copied for Cosimo I from the collection of Paolo Giovio in his palace in Como, were hung on the upper part of the inside wall of the loggia. Others were ordered by the Grand Duke, and later by his successor, to complete the series as far as possible.

The Florentine architect Bernardo Buontalenti constructed the loggia and also the Tribune (now Room 18), which was decorated by Bernardino Poccetti, and remodeled several adjacent rooms in which objects of art and paintings were placed. We have mention of these in an inventory of 1589, made when Francesco was succeeded to the throne by his brother Ferdinando, formerly a cardinal. Among the works listed were the *Portrait of a Young Woman* by Andrea del Sarto, then ascribed to Pontormo; the small tabernacle of Fra Bartolommeo with the *Circumcision* and the *Nativity*, and on the back the *Annunciation*; the *Liberation of Andromeda* by Piero di Cosimo; the two stories of Joseph by Francesco Granacci and those by Andrea del Sarto, now at the Pitti, from the nuptial bedroom of Pierfrancesco Borgherini and Margherita Acciajuoli; *St. John in the Desert* by Raphael; the *Madonna and Child with Little St. John* by Pontormo, then attributed to Andrea del Sarto; the *Taking of Christ* by Sodoma; the so-called *Fornarina*, formerly attributed to Raphael and now recognized as a work of Sebastian del Piombo; the *Deposition* by Gerard David. Many other paintings once exhibited in the Tribune are now in the Pitti, for example, the *St. John the Baptist* by Andrea del Sarto, the *Holy Family* by Domenico Beccafumi, and, by Raphael, the *Madonna dell'Impannata* (*Madonna of the Window*), the *Madonna of the Chair*, and the *Vision of Ezekiel*.

Ferdinando increased the collections of the Gallery considerably by purchasing many ancient sculptures and gathering from everywhere paintings and various rare objects of all sorts. During the short and unhappy government of his successor, Cosimo II (1618–1620), there seems to have been little increase in the size of the collection, but the additions we know about were not without importance. It was during those years that the Tribune was enriched with such paintings as the *Copper Mines* by Henrick Blès, known as Civetta, the *Madonna of St. Zachariah* by Parmigianino, a *Music-Making Putto* by Rosso Fiorentino. Other paintings that we know to have been added to the Gallery include such works as the *Medusa* by

Caravaggio, given to the Grand Duke by Cardinal Anton Maria del Monte in 1608; the *Adoration of the Child* by Correggio, gift of the Duke of Mantua in 1617, and the *Portrait of Sir Richard Southwell* by Hans Holbein the Younger, gift of Thomas Howard, Earl of Arundel, in 1621.

To Cosimo's son Ferdinando II, who reigned from 1621 to 1670, we owe other important improvements. He showed a great interest in continuing and increasing the work started by his ancestors. The Gallery was enlarged and the ceilings of the second and third corridor were decorated with grotesques like those of the first, painted by Cosimo Ulivelli, Jacopo Chiavistelli, and other minor artists. These two corridors were used to accommodate the many additions to the gallery of Classical and contemporary sculptures. Worthy of notice among these are the group of *Bacchus and Ampelos*, an *Aphrodite*, the *Hermaphrodite* purchased by Cardinal Ludovisi, and thirteen Classical heads, among which was the so-called *Head of Cicero*. But still greater was the increase in the number of paintings during the fifty years of Ferdinando II's reign, not only through the frequent purchases and the gifts often sent there, but above all through the legacies from other members of the Ducal family. Some of them had built up formidable collections of their own, such as Don Antonio de' Medici, son of Bianca Cappello, whose works were left to the Grand Duke in 1632; and Cardinal Carlo de' Medici, whose collection entered the Gallery in 1666.

The most important addition of paintings in those years came in 1631 from the Della Rovere family, whose line became extinct with Francesco Maria II, Duke of Urbino and grandfather of Ferdinando's wife Vittoria. The artistic patrimony of the Medici family was notably increased by the legacy, which included such works as the two portraits of Federigo da Montefeltro and Battista Sforza, by Piero della Francesca; by Raphael, a *Self-Portrait* and the portraits of Julius II, Cardinal Dovizi, and Tommaso Inghirami; by Bronzino, the portrait of Guidobaldo della Rovere; by Sebastiano del Piombo, the *Martyrdom of St. Agatha*; by Titian, a very notable group of works, containing the portraits of Francesco Maria della Rovere, Duke of Urbino, and of his wife Eleonora Gonzaga, along with another of an unknown woman called *La Bella*, a male portrait thought to represent the Duke of Norfolk, the *Magdalen*, the *Venus of Urbino*, a half figure of the Saviour, and the *Madonna of the Misericordia*; *Judith*, by Palma Vecchio; and by Baroccio, the portraits of Francesco Maria II della Rovere and of his newly born son Federigo. Some of these paintings now belong to the Uffizi and some to the Pitti.

A year later, in 1632, Don Antonio de' Medici, the son of Bianco Cappello, died, and from the Casino di San Marco where he lived many remarkable works came to the Gallery, such as Mantegna's triptych with the *Adoration of the Magi*, the *Judith* by Botticelli, the *Venus and Cupid* and *Portrait of*

15

Caterina Cornaro by Titian, and two small panels by Fra Angelico, now in the Museum of San Marco. Finally, in 1666, at the death of Cardinal Carlo, other notable works came to the Gallery: the *Entombment* by Rogier van der Weyden and the *Portrait of a Man* (with a medal) by Botticelli, the painting which had belonged to the early Medici collection of the fifteenth century; *Isaiah* by Fra Bartolommeo, the three stories of Andromeda by Piero di Cosimo, the *Madonna of the Well* by Franciabigio, and a Madonna by Pontormo, together with contemporary works such as *Christ and the Pharisees* by Bernardo Strozzi and *Bradamante and Fiordispina* by Guido Reni. Notable additions, other than those derived from the above mentioned bequests, are testified to by the inventories taken during Ferdinando's reign. In 1628 the *Calvary* by Dürer was already in the Gallery; in 1635 the Tribune housed the *Holy Family* by Michelangelo and that by Andrea del Sarto, now at the Pitti, together with *St. Philip*, also by Dürer, *St. George* by Cranach, and the

THE UFFIZI: VIEW FROM ROOM TEN

Portrait of Jacopo Sansovino by Tintoretto; in 1649, in exchange, the *Rest on the Flight to Egypt* by Correggio came from Modena, and finally, in 1670, the *Adoration of the Magi* by Leonardo, which had belonged to Giulio di Don Antonio de' Medici, and a Medusa of the Flemish school, which later was mistakenly attributed to Leonardo.

Cosimo III, successor to Ferdinando II, was responsible for that notable series of seventeenth-century Dutch paintings which still adorn the Gallery. It was further enriched by a collection inherited from Cosimo's uncle, Cardinal Leopoldo, containing besides gems and medals, many self-portraits of artists and a large collection of drawings, which the Grand Duke had Filippo Baldinucci arrange for him. It also included a rich series of paintings from the fifteenth to the seventeenth centuries, among which we find the *Madonna of the Pomegranate* by Botticelli, the *Portrait of an Old Man* by Filippino Lippi, the *Annunciation* by Lorenzo di Credi, the *Immaculate Conception* by Piero di Cosimo, the *Madonna between St. John the Baptist and St. Sebastian* by Perugino, and an exceptional group of Venetian pictures such as the *Knight of Malta* by Giorgione, the *Death of Adonis* and the *Portrait of a Sick Man* by Sebastiano del Piombo, and two portraits by Jacopo Tintoretto, a *Holy Family*, the *Martyrdom of St. Justina,* and two portraits by Paolo Veronese, the *Portrait of His Father* by Dürer, and the *Portrait of the Duchess of Buckingham* by Rubens.

The enlargement of the Gallery, extended to the whole upper floor of the building, allowed also the enlargement of the collection of ancient sculptures, and Cosimo III gathered them from the Boboli, the Pitti, and even from the Villa Pinciana in Rome, where many of them had remained, formerly assembled there by Ferdinando I or purchased later by the Grand Dukes. In this way the Gallery acquired the *Venus de Medici,* the *Knife Grinder,* and the group of the *Wrestlers,* which were immediately placed in the Tribune, where they remain today. The paintings of Cosimo's private collection entered the Gallery before the end of his reign, in 1715, at the death of his son, the great prince Ferdinando. They included works of first importance, such as the *Madonna of St. Mark* by Fra Bartolommeo, the *Madonna of the Harpies* by Andrea del Sarto, *Bacchus* by Guido Reni, the *Nymphs and Satyrs* by Rubens, the *Portrait of Luigi Cornaro* by Tintoretto, and two portraits by Titian.

The reign of the last Medici Grand Duke brought few new works to the Gallery; however, we know that in 1729 the *Dancing Faun* was added to the statues of the Tribune. But when the government passed to the Lorraine family, Anna Maria Lodovica de' Medici, widow of Giovan Guglielmo the Palatine Elector and the last remaining member of the house, declared in a family pact of 1737 that all the art collections of her ancestors should remain in Florence for the enjoyment of the public. The

Gallery, formerly the private property of the Ducal family – though even then it was accessible practically to all – became a public museum, owned by the Tuscan state.

Of the Lorraines who succeeded the Medici, Pietro Leopoldo showed a great interest in the Gallery. He acquired important Classical sculptures from the Gaddi collection, such as the *Torso of a Satyr* and many busts of emperors, and from Rome he obtained the Niobe group, entrusting the arrangement of the room destined for them to Gaspare Paoletti and Grato Albertolli. He continued to remove the most important works from the Medici villa in Rome, such as the so-called *Medici Vase* and the reliefs of the *Ara Pacis Augustae,* now recomposed with others in the reconstructed *Ara* in Rome. The collection of paintings was increased by the addition of a hundred self-portraits to the collection of portraits left by Cardinal Leopoldo; and he enriched the Uffizi with paintings that were formerly scattered not only in the palaces and villas of the Grand Dukes but in the public offices as well. So began the gradual concentration of the works of art in the public galleries, which reached its height in the nineteenth century.

In 1762 a fire destroyed part of the western corridor, but it was immediately repaired and the ceiling redecorated. Pietro Leopoldo was responsible for enlightened reforms in many cultural and political institutions of the Tuscan state. His principal merit regarding our Gallery consists in having promoted a more logical arrangement of the works of art – an arrangement which might be called scientific in the sense we use the term today as applied to museum collection and display. This was brought about by the directors with whom he entrusted the conservation of that great treasure, chief among whom were Raimondo Cocchi, Giuseppe Palli, and Luigi Lanzi. It was due to the intelligent direction of these experts that French paintings were acquired in 1792 in Paris, and that some paintings in the Gallery were advantageously exchanged for others in the Museum of Vienna. In the place of the *Isaiah* by Fra Bartolommeo, the *Madonna and Child with St. John by* Andrea del Sarto, the *Holy Family* by Bronzino, the *St. Luke* by Volterrano, a monk by Baroccio, and the *Madonna and Child* by Dolci, the Gallery acquired ten paintings, which include such works as the *Sacred Allegory* by Giovanni Bellini, the *Madonna and Child with St. John the Baptist and St. Anthony Abbot* and *Flora* by Titian, the *Herodiade* by Luini, the *Holy Family* by Palma Vecchio, *Esther and Ahasuerus* by Paolo Veronese and the *Adoration of the Magi* by Dürer.

The period of the French domination of Italy marked the exodus of many works of art from the Florentine Gallery: the *Venus de Medici* had been sent to Paris by 1799, together with many works from the Pitti, to which more spoils were added in 1810. The city never recovered all its losses after the fall of Napoleon. The Gallery soon began steadily improving its arrangement, principally by separating the paintings from other works of art – sculptures, medals, drawings, majolicas, etc. – until then all exhibited together. Because of subsequent additions to the collection, particularly of archeological material, new museums had to be created, one of which is the present Archeological Museum in the Palazzo della Crocetta. The National Museum, known also as the Bargello, founded in 1865 and housed in the Palazzo del Podesta, accommodated medieval and Renaissance sculpture and objects of the minor arts, so that only paintings and Classical sculpture remained in the Uffizi. In this way the Gallery has gradually succeeded in obtaining its present character, and has collected many other works from the churches of the suppressed monasteries and convents or from important purchases, such as the acquisition of the gallery of the Hospital of Santa Maria Nuova, of which the famous *Portinari Triptych* by Hugo van der Goes was a part.

Though the cream of the Medici collection was housed in the Uffizi, many works remained in their private homes. The Pitti Palace was acquired for the Medici family by Cosimo I, who soon took up residence there, and its rooms – just as formerly in the Palazzo Vecchio and in the family's other residences – were adorned little by little with paintings, statues, and other precious objects, some of which later entered the Uffizi, often in exchange for other works. Within a century this collection had grown so large that toward the end of the reign of Cosimo II it was decided to exhibit the works together in a few rooms of the Pitti Palace, thus constituting a private Grand Ducal gallery. This first group was considerably augmented by Ferdinando II, who around the year 1640 commissioned frescoes for five large rooms in one of the apartments on the first floor, with the intention of arranging his own gallery there. During this time Alfonso Parigi was engaged in the construction of the wings of the Palace, which give it its present monumentality. The decoration of the rooms was entrusted to one of the most talented artists of the period, noted especially for this type of painting: Pietro da Cortona. Assisted by his pupil Ciro Ferri, he succeeded in creating a sumptuous yet solemn interior. It is one of the few princely galleries of that time which remain to us. The ceilings painted by these two artists were also decorated with stucco figures and gilt friezes, which gave a still greater splendor to the rooms, each of which is named for a divinity or a planet. They allude to the principal virtues attributed to Cosimo I, of whom this ensemble constitutes a kind of glorification. Venus signifies his goodness, Apollo his magnificence, Mars the force of his laws, Jupiter his majesty and the reward of merit, Saturn his prudence and depth of knowledge. The idea was a creation of Michelangelo Buonarroti the Younger, poet and man of letters who was highly esteemed by his contemporaries. The walls were

19

covered with rich brocades and on them were hung the Grand Duke's favorite pictures.

Of the two great collections, the Uffizi Gallery was open to all visitors, Italian and foreign, many of whom left us descriptions, interesting not only for their historical content, but primarily for the insight they give us on the fluctuations of taste. The importance they give to certain works and their judgement on them are especially revealing. Such visitors were: John Evelyn, Balthasar de Monconys, Richard Lassels, Joseph Addison, Jerome de la Lande. The Pitti, on the other hand, remained until the end of the eighteenth century an exclusively private collection of the Grand Duke, and was shown only to those who had the honor of being guests of the prince. In 1798 it was arranged more like a museum: to the five rooms, decorated in the seventeenth-century fashion already mentioned, others were added until there were nearly twenty rooms. Some masterpieces were placed again in the Uffizi, such as the *Portrait of Pope Leo X with the Cardinals Giulio de' Medici and Luigi de' Rossi* and the *Madonna of the Chair* by Raphael; other important works came permanently to the Palace, such as the many Flemish paintings received from the last Medici legacy – of Anna Maria Ludovica, the Palatine Electress, and those purchased by Francesco II, the first of the Lorraine grand dukes. There was also the group of paintings acquired by the Pitti from the Marchesi Gerini, containing among others a Van Dyck, two Salvator Rosas, and a *Self-Portrait* by Rembrandt. This was the last acquisition of Ferdinando II, made in 1818. He is to be remembered principally for having purchased the *Madonna of the Grand Duke* by Raphael. Some time later Leopold II added Raphael's portraits of Agnolo and Maddalena Doni, for whose marriage Michelangelo had painted the *Holy Family* now in the Uffizi. In the nineteenth century the Pitti, which had contained paintings exclusively, was enriched by some late works of sculpture, such as the *Venus* by Canova (which replaced the *Venus de Medici* at the Uffizi when it was taken to Paris), followed later by the *Charity* of Lorenzo Barolini and other works.

*   *   *   *

In its present form the Uffizi is principally, if not exclusively, a gallery of paintings which shows the development of Italian painting from its origins in the thirteenth century, to the eighteenth; at the same time, the Uffizi documents the principal accomplishments of other European schools, though here there are some important omissions.

Of the early Italian paintings now in the Uffizi, few were in any way connected with the numerous Medici collections which form the substance of the Gallery. This is not surprising since from the sixteenth century onward, Italian taste—as well as European taste in general—exalted the classical

1

FRA FILIPPO LIPPI : *Florentine/c. 1406–1469/*THE MADONNA AND CHILD WITH SCENES FROM THE LIFE OF THE VIRGIN/*Circular panel/Diameter 53⅛″/Pitti*

This *tondo*, or round panel, certainly painted in the last period of the Friar's sojourn in Prato, can probably be dated 1452, and has been identified by some students as the one painted that year for Leonardo Bartolini. It is among the most perfect works of the artist. The intense, motherly feeling which animates the Madonna reminds us of Donatello or Desiderio da Settignano. In her face is that deeply human beauty found in all of Lippi's figures. But especially wonderful is the composition, for the perfect coherence with which the scenes from the Virgin's life, in the background, harmonize with the main subject in the foreground; they do not at all disturb the solemnity of the principal group. And in those scenes we already find motifs that will again appear with other painters of the second half of the *quattrocento*: for example, the very pretty girl bearing a basket on her head, who presages Botticelli and is repeated by Domenico Ghirlandaio in his frescoes at Santa Maria Novella. The round shape of the painting had already been used by Lippi in another admirable picture, the *Adoration of the Magi* in the National Gallery of Art, at Washington.

achievement of the *cinquecento* to the detriment of the earlier masters, who were even berated for their "primitive" and "imperfect" styles. For example, Giorgio Vasari in his *Lives of the Most Eminent Painters* (which was first published in 1550, and in 1568 appeared in a much expanded form) reserved most of his admiration for those artists who, in his opinion, most closely approached the ideals of his own art (which was closer to Michelangelo than to Raphael). But, true artist and connoisseur that he was, he did not fail to appreciate the work of earlier centuries.

A variety of events was responsible for the formation of this nucleus of early Italian paintings. Many were removed from churches during the extensive remodeling of altars that took place during the sixteenth century; the altars in Santa Croce and Santa Maria Novella, for example, were modernized by Vasari. The Medici, in their enthusiasm for collecting, took a few paintings from the churches to enhance their own private collections. But much more important than this was the suppression and confiscation of property suffered by many religious orders under Pietro Leopoldo of Lorraine, under Napoleon, and in the early years of the Kingdom of Italy. The paintings acquired from these suppressed convents originally formed the collection of the Gallery of the Accademia di Belle Arti (Academy of Fine Arts), and did not enter the Uffizi until 1919, with some of the greatest treasures now in our Gallery. The gallery of the Accademia is now a subsidiary of the Uffizi.

Two works of the Lucchese school are among the earliest examples of Tuscan painting, which in its first days tended to assimilate the forms of Byzantine painting. These are a diptych of a *Christ on the Cross* and a *Madonna and Child* in the manner of Bonaventura Berlinghieri, and a *Stigmatization of St. Francis,* attributable perhaps to the same hand because of a certain subtle stylization of form and color. The Florentine school is represented by two painted crucifixes still somewhat crude in their imitation of the Byzantine manner, harsh in color and ungainly in composition. The large altarpiece painted in 1271 by the Florentine Meliore di Jacopo, which hangs near these works, is still a far cry from the manner of Cimabue, who is considered to have been the regenerator of painting—not only in Florence but in all Italy.

The *Madonna and Child with Saints* from the church of Santa Trinita has always been considered the most important work by Cimabue. Though still Byzantine in composition, forms, soft color, and light, it is already pervaded with that plasticity which subsequently became the essential characteristic of Florentine art. Here we see how the form and drawing predominate over color. Dante's praise of the artist in the *Divine Comedy* — that he "held the field in painting before Giotto" — is fully justified in this Madonna with its monumental conception and its vividly dramatic

22

presence. The vitalization of painting begun by Cimabue was accomplished by Giotto who, before he matured, probably followed the style of Cimabue, as is testified by tradition and the character of some of his early works. The *Madonna* in the Uffizi, which comes from the church of Ognissanti and has long been attributed to Giotto, belongs to his mature period. The natural postures of the angels – who, no longer present as mere decorative ornaments, take an active part in the scene – and the firm modeling of the faces, especially in the Madonna, give a new life to the traditional scheme of this composition. The third early *Madonna and Child with Angels* in the Uffizi, the so-called "Rucellai Madonna," also drew its inspiration from Cimabue, but with entirely different results. This work is generally considered to be the painting executed by Duccio di Buoninsegna in 1285 for the church of Santa Maria Novella, from where it is now temporarily on loan to the Uffizi. Duccio was Sienese, and as such, he combined Sienese traits with the influence of Cimabue, as we may see in the delicate grace of his composition and in the lovely colors of this work.

The Sienese school is represented in the Gallery by one of its most outstanding works, the *Annunciation* by Simone Martini. Gothic style is at its most splendid in this painting with its wonderful rhythms of line and its wonderful, abstract color. The paintings of the Sienese Pietro and Ambrogio Lorenzetti are fitting companions to this work. Pietro's *Madonna in Glory* and his altarpiece of *Scenes from the Life of St. Humility* richly reflect the artist's contacts with the art of Giotto. In the *Scenes from the Life of St. Nicholas* and the *Presentation in the Temple* by Ambrogio, the perspective researches of the artist are incorporated, as it were, in the over-all pictorial effect.

The majority of our fourteenth-century paintings belongs of course to the Florentine school, and they clearly illustrate the influence Giotto had on his contemporaries and his early followers. These paintings include the panel of *Scenes from the Life of St. Cecilia* by a master who later collaborated with Giotto in the famous frescoes in the church of St. Francis at Assisi; the *Madonna* by Taddeo Gaddi, who was even more Gothic in style than his master; and the Madonnas by Bernardo Daddi, who became increasingly sensitive to the influence of Siena, as we can see in the softness of his modeling and even more in his tendency toward Gothic. Jacopo del Casentino contributes a small domestic diptych, donated to the Gallery by Guido Cagnola, and a *St. Bartholomew*. The *Deposition* from the church of San Remigio, the authorship of which is still subject for debate, continues in the direct tradition of Giotto even more than the preceding works.

The late *trecento* (fourteenth century) marked the beginning of the International Gothic style which lasted through the early *quattrocento* (fifteenth century). In our Gallery this style is represented by the *Thebaid* of Gherardo Starnina and by the works of Lorenzo Monaco, whose principal work here is the large *Coronation of the Virgin* in which Sienese Gothic is combined with a power of modeling completely Florentine. The influence of Giotto on Lombard painting can be seen in the works of Giovanni da Milano, whose series of saints now in the Uffizi came from a large altarpiece painted for the high altar of the church of Ognissanti.

In the early fifteenth century one painter stands out as the Renaissance unfolds: Fra Giovanni da Fiesole, the Dominican monk known as Fra Angelico. He has left us incomparable examples of his art in the Florentine Convent of San Marco — a wonderful series of frescoes near which are gathered almost all his works that remain in Florence. In the Uffizi he is represented by a panel of the *Coronation of the Virgin,* of resplendent spiritual vigor, and a *Madonna and Child* from a church of Pontassieve. In the *Coronation* the exalted mysticism of Angelico's earlier works is combined with traits of the new style which was beginning to prevail in Florence, while in the *Madonna and Child* the artist obtains a perfect synthesis of medieval and Renaissance.

Renaissance painting has its original and almost perfect expression in Masaccio's *Madonna and Child with St. Anne,* one of the few works by this supreme artist, who left in his frescoes at the church of the Carmine in Florence what was perhaps the greatest single inspiration for the entire Renaissance. Nothing is more eloquent in revealing Masaccio's artistic personality than to observe how, with a background which must have been essentially Gothic, there is in this early painting a renewal of that true Italian tradition which had found its first concrete expression in Giotto.

In Florence, at this moment, a tendency to picture the visible world in a more natural manner was becoming dominant. A short stay in that city was sufficient to have notable effect on the work of a painter like Gentile da Fabriano, who was thoroughly saturated with the spirit of the fourteenth-century International Gothic style. His masterpiece of this period is the resplendent *Adoration of the Magi* in the Uffizi. The teaching of Brunelleschi and of the sculptor Donatello, so essential in Masaccio, was quickly finding further new expression in Masaccio's immediate followers. Paolo Uccello, in the *Battle of San Romano,* applies his masters' principles of perspective to great effect. Domenico Veneziano, as we may see in his Uffizi panel, creates an atmospheric perspective through an original feeling for color. Fra Filippo Lippi reflects the influence of both Fra Angelico and Masaccio, but it was principally to the latter that Lippi was most indebted since he belonged to the Convent of the Carmine where he could see the great works which Masaccio had painted there. Lippi's two Nativities in the Uffizi attest his search for a handling of forms and figures that was freer than that characteristic of even his early works. His pictorial conceptions and the

24

amplitude of his figures derive from Masaccio. The predella of an altarpiece formerly in the church of Santo Spirito, of which we have the fragments at the Uffizi, is an example of the full development of his art, as is also the *Madonna* painted for the Medici chapel in Santa Croce, with its intense feeling for realistic setting. We see this too in the even more famous *Coronation of the Virgin*, in the *tondo* at the Pitti, and in the *Madonna and Child with Angels* at the Uffizi. In the predella of the Santa Croce *Madonna*, Lippi's pupil Francesco Pesellino reminds us of Angelico as well as of his master, and, through him, of Masaccio. Piero della Francesca united the experiences of the closest followers of Angelico, of Masolino, and of Masaccio. His only remaining work in Florence is the diptych in the Uffizi, since the frescoes painted in collaboration with Domencio Veneziano in the church of Sant'Egidio are now lost. The two portraits of Federigo da Montefeltro and of his wife Battista Sforza are a testimonial of his perfect simplicity, while the two Triumphs on the reverse side fascinate us by the splendor of their color and light, a characteristic of his art.

Piero and Alesso Baldovinetti mark the passage between the first and the second half of the *quattrocento* in Florence. Baldovinetti's *Annunciation* still reflects the work of Angelico and Domenico Veneziano, though in his *Sacred Conversation* the influence of Andrea del Castagno's plastic energy is apparent. Piero Pollaiuolo and his brother Antonio achieve a fusion of pictorial and sculptural forms in the *Altarpiece of the Three Saints*, from the church of San Miniato al Monte. The *Virtues*, six panels painted by Piero for the Palazzo di Mercanzia, show the influence of Antonio; here Piero does not fail to equal the force of his brother's work, evident, for example, though marred by several repaintings, in the female portrait at the Uffizi, especially when compared to Piero's *Portrait of Galeazzo Maria Sforza*.

Sandro Botticelli studied with Filippo Lippi, whose influence is evident in his earliest works, though there is added a charm and a humanity which is Botticelli's own. Some of his early works in the Uffizi are the *Madonna of the Rose-Hedge*, the figure of *Fortitude*, which completes the above mentioned *Six Virtues* by Piero Pollaiuolo, and the *Madonna of the Loggia*. But under the influence of Antonio Pollaiuolo and Verrocchio, Botticelli's work soon took on new strength, as we can see in the two small pictures from the story of Judith, and in the *Portrait of a Man* holding the medal of Cosimo the Elder. His aristic personality is fully expressed in the *Adoration of the Magi*, and triumphs in the *Primavera*, where his usual vigorous modeling is combined with a transparency of forms, attaining an expression of sweetness veiled with melancholy. Even more splendid than the *Primavera*, though very delicate, are the two *tondi*, the *Madonna of the Magnificat* and the *Madonna of the Pomegranate*, and still more vigorous, the *Madonna* originally painted for the church of St. Barnabas, with its

25

2

BOTTICELLI : *Florentine/1444:5–1510/*PRIMAVERA*/Panel/ 79⅞ x 123⅝″/Uffizi*

Painted between 1477 and 1480 for Lorenzo di Pier Francesco's villa of Castello near Florence. This is one of the most beautiful interpretations of a classical vision. Though, like the *Birth of Venus* (plate 31) its subject may have been suggested to the artist by Angelo Poliziano, it also derives inspiration from Lucretius, Horace, and Ovid.

Some critics have tried to identify certain figures with personages in the Medici family or have regarded the entire scene as referring to an event connected with that family. Whether this is true or not, it adds nothing to the artist's creative power and capacity for poetic expression. In this composition, unified by the linear rhythm of its figures which suavely express grace and lightness without any loss of energy, Botticelli reveals the dominant influence of Antonio del Pollaiuolo. The types, somewhat different from those habitual to the artist, have a quality at once human and superhuman, which accords perfectly with the dreamlike mood that pervades the entire work.

From the Grand-Ducal *guardaroba* the painting passed to the Accademia in 1853 and thence in 1919 to the Uffizi.

beautiful predella panels. His spontaneous idealization of forms can be seen in *Pallas and the Centaur*, and in the *Birth of Venus*, a true hymn to beauty pervaded with a deeply religious feeling despite the secular nature of the subject. The *Calumny of Apelles* and the *Annunciation* give us a hint of the artist's spiritual inquietude during the last period of his life, while the *Coronation of the Virgin* shows his search for monumentality in composition.

Filippino Lippi appears as the faithful pupil of Botticelli in his *Madonna and Child with Saints* at the Uffizi, actually a Sacred Conversation painted for the Signoria of Florence, in which he achieves a perfect unity of the whole. Perfectly harmonious is the *Adoration of the Magi,* painted to replace the one left unfinished by Leonardo; here Filippino reveals the influence of the *Portinari Triptych* by Hugo van der Goes, which had been sent to Florence in the last decades of the century. Other painters show this same influence at the close of the century: Piero di Cosimo, in his *Immaculate Conception,* where the figures are of outstanding naturalistic power, and in the still more decorative panels with the story of Andromeda; Domenico Ghirlandaio, whose youthful *Madonna Enthroned* also shows the influence of Verrocchio, while his later Madonna has a plastic grandeur which is not to be found in the pleasing and more descriptive *tondo* of the *Adoration of the Magi.* Powerful modeling is particularly evident in the *Baptism of Christ* by Andrea del Verrocchio, which still reflects the forms of Baldovinetti, though here the artist reveals a dignity and grandeur of his own, well in keeping with the intense spirituality of the angel at the left of the painting, traditionally said to have been painted by Leonardo. Other artists influenced by Verrocchio were Francesco Botticini, whose *Tobias and the Three Archangels* at the Uffizi, though graceful, seems somewhat contrived; and Lorenzo di Credi, a collaborator and follower of the master, and author of the lovely *Annunciation* at the Uffizi with the three scenes from Genesis in the predella, and of the *Adoration of the Shepherds,* a more naturalistic and monumental composition. It was in this milieu that Leonardo da Vinci developed, and soon, in his *Annunciation,* he transformed and improved the forms of traditional composition; later, with the *Adoration of the Magi,* he achieved a powerful dramatic feeling, where the event is portrayed in heroic proportions.

Two of the greatest artists of the end of the century, Luca Signorelli and Pietro Perugino, though not Florentine, were nonetheless attracted by the new ideals of Florentine art. They probably came from the school of Piero della Francesca, and soon reached Florence. We have in the Uffizi one of Signorelli's best works, the circular panel of the *Holy Family,* which is monumental in composition and in the sculptural power of forms. Perugino's notable works are in both the Uffizi and the Pitti. The Uffizi now houses the lovely *Portrait of a Youth,* who is perhaps Alessandro Braccesi, later

secretary to a magistracy in the Florentine Republic; the *Pietà*, so skillful in execution, which still reflects the teaching of Piero della Francesca; the *Madonna between St. John the Baptist and St. Sebastian*, sublime in its religious feeling; the vigorous *Portrait of Francesco delle Opere*, and the two portraits of Vallombrosan monks. The *Deposition*, a work of his mature years, admirable for the expression of the faces and the airy and poetical landscape in the background, is in the Pitti.

The example of Florence also brought the idea of the Renaissance among the artists of Northern Italy. The first to embrace this new style was Andrea Mantegna, whose precious triptych is preserved in the Uffizi. Some have identified this work with the one seen by Vasari in the chapel of the Gonzaga palace in Mantua. In this notable work, all the pictorial qualities of the artist are revealed; the monumentality of composition is not at all diminished by the fine, almost miniature-like execution. More naturalistic is perhaps the *Portrait of a Gonzaga*, also in the Uffizi, whose vigorous expression shows a firm and rude temperament; more lovely and graceful, like other paintings of the last period of his life, is the *Madonna of the Caves*, where the Virgin and Child stand out against a background of rocks. The founder of the Ferrarese school of painting, Cosimo Tura, was strongly influenced by Mantegna and Piero della Francesca; his *St. Dominic* in the Uffizi belongs to a polyptych which has been broken up and scattered in various museums in Italy and abroad. It is one of Tura's late works, in which he shows a tendency to accentuate the expressive quality of the figure and to distort the forms, while renouncing all attempts at obtaining a decorative effect. Lorenzo Costa, a pupil of Tura, is represented in the Gallery by the *Portrait of Giovanni II Bentivoglio*, executed in the late fifteenth century. In this work he no longer adheres to the forms of his master, but rather tends toward a more vigorous modeling, perhaps under the influence of another Ferrarese, Ercole de' Roberti, an influence which was later weakened, as appears from the somewhat conventional half length of *St. Sebastian*, a painting which reminds us of the Bolognese Francesco Francia. The *Portrait of Evangelista Scappi* was painted while Francia was still under the influence of Perugino; there was an altarpiece by Perugino in the Bolognese church of San Giovanni in Monte which Francia doubtlessly knew well. The portrait is frank, the colors soft; it is already *cinquecento* (sixteenth century) in style, as is the majority of the works of his followers, of whom we may cite here the *Holy Family* signed by Jacopo de' Boateri, in the Pitti.

Equally ready to accept the new Renaissance forms were the Venetian painters, first of all Jacopo Bellini, a pupil of Gentile da Fabriano, and above all his son Giovanni. We have a masterpiece by Giovanni in the Uffizi, the *Sacred Allegory*, which in the fanciful landscape full of deep poetry, and in the perfect harmony of elements of the composition, perhaps marks the apex of the artist's formation. The *Pietà* in grisaille is no less remarkable for its monumental conception. Bellini's *Portrait of a Man* is of a slightly later period. Unfortunately we have few examples of the other Venetian painters of the late *quattrocento*. They are represented only by a *Sacred Conversation* by the mediocre painter Pietro Duja, a follower of Vincenzo Catena, and by a *Group of Halberdiers* from a Crucifixion by Vittore Carpaccio, which is quite close to his famous cycle of St. Ursula in the gallery of the Accademia in Venice. The Lombards are also represented by few important works: the *Zingarella* by Boccaccio Boccaccino of Cremona, who was more or less influenced by the Venetian style, and, among others, the small *Madonna and Child* by Cima da Conegliano. One of Leonardo's Milanese followers is Boltraffio, whose idealized head of *Narcissus* is painted with delicate sensibility. Boltraffio is a painter still faithful to the *quattrocento* aesthetic, just as Leonardo's other followers in Milan, who, though without assimilating the true substance of his art, nevertheless opened the way to a new pictorial vision.

Leonardo is still very close to the forms of his master Verrocchio in the figure of the angel presumed to have been painted by him in Verrocchio's *Baptism*, as well as in the *Annunciation* in the Uffizi. But this latter work already bears the signs of the great artist's originality in the stately figure of the Virgin and in the broad and varied landscape before which the scene of the Annunciation is set. His artistic personality is fully manifested in the *Adoration of the Magi*, where space fades away in the distance and light is the principal element of the composition, the whole animated by the vibrating architectural forms and by the figures crowded around the main group. The light is centered on the Madonna and Child to enhance the splendor of the divine pair in contrast with the other

3

BOTTICELLI : *Florentine/1444:5–1510/*THE RETURN OF JUDITH*/Panel/12¼ x 9½"/Uffizi*

The figure of Judith, like that of David, was a favorite subject of Florentine artists of the *quattrocento*, who saw symbols of liberty in these biblical heroes. Originally this little painting formed a diptych with a companion piece representing the tent of Holofernes. The panels were presented by Rodolfo Sirigatti to Bianco Capello, wife of Francesco I de' Medici, and inherited by her son, Don Antonio de' Medici, who left his collection to the Gallery in 1632. A replica, generally regarded as a school piece but nevertheless of very high quality, was formerly in the collection of the Prince of Fondi at Naples, and went from the Bardini Collection to the Cincinnati Art Museum.

The painting, probably executed shortly after 1470, is noteworthy for its intensely dramatic expressiveness combined with elegant forms and vivid coloring. It reveals Botticelli's decided predilection for the dynamic linear style of Antonio del Pollaiuolo.

participants of the scene who are enveloped in a shadow which is brightened with sparkling reflections.

Fra Bartolommeo, who was the first representative in Florence of Leonardo's pictorial reform, had not yet felt his influence in the small tabernacle at the Uffizi with the *Annunciation*, the *Circumcision*, and the *Nativity*; he shows the influence of Michelangelo in the *St. Mark* of the Pitti. His great personality is revealed in the *Deposition* of the same gallery, a masterpiece of perfect compositional equilibrium and chromatic splendor, expressing a profound feeling of love. More intensely Michelangelesque is the *Risen Christ*, also in the Pitti, where there is also a *Holy Family* which documents the last period of the painter's activity, a period much less vigorously inspired than his earlier works. Mariotto Albertinelli, Fra Bartolommeo's assistant, is still close to the art of Piero di Cosimo in the *tondo* at the Pitti of the *Adoration of the Child*; while in the *Visitation* at the Uffizi he reveals the influence of Fra Bartolommeo in the conception of the picture, in the proportions of the figures, and in the grandeur of the somewhat simple scene, though, in the predella the traditions of the *quattrocento* are still evident. The female portrait, known as the *Nun of Leonardo* owing to its former attribution, might be by Albertinelli, judging principally from the landscape in the background. Today the work is generally attributed to Giuliano Bugiardini, a colorist of the Florentine school of the early *cinquecento*, but he is generally inferior to the author of this portrait, intense yet delicate and exquisitely painted, though rather cold in the tones of color.

Raphael's influence can be seen in the *Portrait of a Youth* by Franciabigio at the Uffizi, though the landscape and face remind us of Fra Bartolommeo. Bachiacca, another Florentine painter of the early sixteenth century, was largely influenced by Umbrian painting. His *Deposition* and the predella with *Scenes from the Life of St. Acacius* reveal the artist's bizarre genius; the *St. Mary Magdalen* of the Pitti is a subtle and precious portrayal of a female type. There is a particular brightness and elegance in the paintings of Francesco Granacci; in the Joseph stories at the Uffizi, though minutely attentive to details, he obtains a clear definition of space. These same virtues are to be found in his fellow pupil Ridolfo del Ghirlandaio, whose *Portrait of a Goldsmith* in the Pitti is worthy of mention. Today some critics accept the former attribution of this work to Leonardo, due to the undeniable traits of the master in the picture, though these can probably be explained by the eclecticism of the majority of the minor artists of that period, so strongly influenced by their great contemporaries that their own artistic personalities are not always clear.

An exception was Andrea del Sarto, an extradorinary figure who at this time was beginning to rise above all these minor artists. Though strongly influenced by Leonardo and especially by Raphael, Andrea remains highly original in all his works. Among his earliest paintings are the two Annunciations in the Pitti, in which there are echoes of Raphael and of Fra Bartolommeo; but his forms have a solidity and fullness of their own that were typical of the artist, and are also to be found in the somewhat later *Portrait of a Young Woman* at the Uffizi, in which the precious color is absorbed by the atmosphere with a mastery which reveals the extraordinary pictorial talent of the artist at its height. Immediately afterward, when Andrea was still working in the Chiostro dello Scalzo, we can place the *Madonna of the Harpies,* a bold composition enveloped in a golden atmosphere and embellished with touches of precious color. With the exception of his frescoes, this is perhaps Andrea's greatest masterpiece. The so-called *Self-Portrait* of the Pitti belongs to about the same period, and we can date as shortly afterward the *Dispute on the Holy Trinity,* also in the Pitti, where the influence of Leonardo in composition and color and that of Michelangelo in the forms are fused to create a work of pensive austerity. The two Assumptions of the Virgin and the *Deposition* of the Pitti are perhaps less successful, though in the latter there is originality in the dramatic conception of the composition, and the quality of the drawing is excellent; of the Assumptions, one is particularly interesting due to its perfect execution and delicacy of tints. A better work is the lovely *Annunciation,* originally part of an altarpiece now in Berlin and contemporary with the panel of the *Four Saints* in the Uffizi. It is rich in coloring and painted with wonderful skill; the two little angels holding scrolls placed nearby belong to this work. Among the works of this period we have his *Self-Portrait* in the Uffizi painted on a tile, "so naturally and to such perfection, that one might almost believe him to be in life," as Vasari has described it. To the artist's last years belong the two Holy Families in the Pitti, of which the one executed for Ottaviano de' Medici is particularly excellent in the harmony of composition and the grace of features, as well as in the perfect fusion of each color in the atmosphere enveloping the scene. The statuesque *St. John the Baptist* in the same gallery, and the standard for the Compagnia di San Jacopo del Nicchio, *St. James with Two Children,* at the Uffizi also belong to these years.

We have often mentioned Michelangelo's influence on the Florentine painters of the early *cinquecento,* an influence which was naturally exercised by the personality of Michelangelo through his works of both sculpture and painting. The *Holy Family* in the Uffizi, painted for the marriage of Agnolo Doni and Maddalena Strozzi, is the earliest painting known by Michelangelo, yet his entire artistic personality and his preponderantly plastic vision is mirrored in it. We notice particularly the perfect composition of the masses, the energy which emanates from the central group, in which the attitudes of the figures are balanced in a powerful whole, and the color, which heightens the modeling of the marble-like forms.

No less strong was the influence exercised by Raphael on the Florentine painters, especially during his sojourns in Florence before he was called to Rome. We have many examples in our galleries of this period, in which the artist combined the styles of Umbria and Florence. The perfect harmony of its simple composition is the greatest merit of the so-called *Madonna of the Grand Duke* in the Pitti. The two Doni portraits in the same room constitute the prototype of the Florentine portrait in the early *cinquecento*, and were influenced to some degree by Leonardo's *Mona Lisa*; together with the portrait called *La Gravida* (*The Pregnant Woman*), perhaps slightly earlier, they demonstrate a perfect unity of spirit and form. In each of these portraits the character of the individual subject is abstracted to form the image of a universal human type. The formation of Raphael's artistic personality is now complete. Even more typically Florentine is the *Madonna of the Goldfinch*, a supreme expression of spiritual values notwithstanding the profound humanity of the figures, which stand out from the landscape immediately surrounding them. The *Madonna del Baldacchino* (*Madonna of the Canopy*) in the Pitti, the last work of this period, recalls contemporary Florentine compositions, though with more movement. Raphael's Roman period is represented in the Florentine galleries by a series of wonderful portraits: of Tommaso Inghirami and of Cardinal Bibbiena in the Pitti, the powerful one of Pope Julius II in the Uffizi, and, again in the Pitti, the *Donna Velata* or *Portrait of a Veiled Woman*, wonderful in its powerful coloring and idealized type, and in the stupendous symphony of the silky dress. Slightly later is the small picture of the *Vision of Ezekiel* in the Pitti, a monumental composition, and the famous *Madonna of the Chair*, where it is principally the feeling of human motherhood that is evident. A masterpiece of the artist's last period is the *Portrait of Pope Leo X with the Cardinals Giulio de' Medici and Luigi de' Rossi*, showing an extraordinary power in the plastic construction of the figures and in the architectural unity of the group. Raphael's pupils collaborated with their master in many of his works. Suffice it to mention here the *Madonna dell'Impannata* in the Pitti, where only the composition and drawing are by Raphael, and even that was altered somewhat by the man who actually painted the picture.

Correggio was another notable *cinquecento* painter influenced by the works of Leonardo, Raphael, and Michelangelo, but he assimilated their teachings in a quite original way, attaining a completely personal art. The little *Virgin in Glory* in the Uffizi still recalls Mantegna as well as his early training in Ferrara, while the *Rest on the Flight to Egypt*, set in a lovely wooded landscape, though influenced by Raphael to some extent,

4

RAPHAEL : *Central Italian/1483–1520/*THE MADONNA OF THE GOLDFINCH*/Panel/ 42⅛ x 30¼″/Uffizi*

Painted for the Florentine Lorenzo Nasi around 1506, it belongs to the beginning of the second Florentine period of the artist, when the influence of Tuscany was blended with the spirit and forms of his Umbrian sources. The beautiful integration of the figures and the landscape background gives a greater life and humanity to the scene. The pyramidal form of the Madonna and Child is derived from Fra Bartolommeo and Leonardo, but the particular fascination of the work comes above all from the sublime loveliness of the faces.

gives us an original interpretation of the subject, accentuated by the artist's characteristic diagonal composition. In the *Adoration of the Child* the artist attains effects of exquisite charm both in composition and in color.

Parmigianino's style was formed by the works of Correggio, but he too was influenced by Raphael, as we can see in the *Madonna of St. Zachariah* in the Uffizi. He later attained a particular mannerism of his own in the *Madonna with the Long Neck,* which represents the culmination of his aesthetic, directed toward a formal perfection of style. The result is often cold, but his portraits, like the one in the Uffizi formerly considered to be a self-portrait, are considerably more sensitive. Sodoma was influenced particularly by Leonardo; in his *St. Sebastian* at the Pitti we have one of his more studied works, with graceful shadows which envelope the figure, and a landscape which fades away in the distance.

Venetian painting of the *cinquecento* is well represented in the two Florentine galleries, due principally to the large collection left to the Medici by the Della Rovere family of Urbino. Attributable without doubt to Giorgione are the panels of the *Trial of Moses* and the *Judgment of Solomon,* youthful works which both in figures and landscape reveal to us all the characteristic elements of the artist. The *Warrior with Shield-Bearer* is perhaps a replica after a lost original by Giorgione, though it is generally attributed to Cavazzola, while the painting in the Pitti known as the *Three Ages of Man* is probably authentic, for the novelty and originality of its composition and for the Giorgionesque character of that silent conversation; the much discussed *Knight of Malta* in the Uffizi is in all probability also his, and though a later work, it still conforms to Giorgione's own ideal of beauty.

Sebastiano del Piombo was influenced by Giorgione in the so-called *Portrait of the Sick Man* at the Uffizi, painted when he was already in Rome, though a recent suggestion has been made that Titian and not Sebastiano was the author of this masterpiece. Sebastiano's *Portrait of a Lady* in the Uffizi, at one time thought to be Raphael's *La Fornarina,* certainly recalls the style of his Umbrian contemporary, while the formal principles of Michelangelo are more closely followed in the *Martryrdom of St. Agatha* of the Pitti, rich in its splendid Venetian color, and in the *Portrait of Baccio Valori,* also in the Pitti, admirable not only for the power of the brushwork and modeling, but also for the relief obtained by the light which illuminates the subject's face.

The works of Titian follow directly from those of Giorgione. We see this in the *Madonna of the Roses* in the Uffizi, and still more in the *Concert* at the Pitti—for so long a time attributed to Giorgione himself—a

5

TITIAN : *Venetian/1490?–1576/*VENUS OF URBINO/*Canvas/65 x 76¾"/Uffizi*

Painted around 1538, the picture had been left in Titian's shop, and Guidobaldo della Rovere, later Duke of Urbino, demanded it. Vasari saw the painting in the Duke's *guardaroba*, and describes it as "a young Venus reclining, amidst flowers and sheer fabrics, very beautifully and well finished." It is quite possibly the portrait of a favorite of the Duke; at any rate she is the same person as the model in *La Bella* (plate 74), and in the young woman with fur at the Museum of Vienna. This nude is no longer detached and chaste, like those of Giorgione. Here the woman is conscious of—and even pleased with—her own nude beauty. The body is modeled with extraordinary skill, and the face is ideally beautiful. The bed, the sheet, and the drapery against which the ripe body of Venus stands out, all constitute a most felicitous ensemble of colors. The work came to Florence in 1631 with the Della Rovere collection.

masterpiece of that period of the artist, and in the *Portrait of Tommaso Mosti,* also in the Pitti, nor far removed from the musician of the *Concert* for the intense expression of his gaze and attitude. The *Flora* in the Uffizi is a more completely personal work by Titian, revealing that ideal of feminine beauty he created, as are the portraits painted shortly afterward, like *La Bella* in the Pitti. There is certainly an interpretation of the sitter's personality in this portrait, though the artist's principal means here of transforming the concrete reality of his subject into art is to be found in his use of color. The same person was the model for the *Venus of Urbino* at the Uffizi, whose light and soft body with its delicate coloring nobly represent the goddess of beauty; here Titian "modernizes" the traditional conception of Venus without spoiling at all her divine charm. The same vagueness of forms and an increasing vibration of light are attained in the *Portrait of Cardinal Ippolito de' Medici* in the Pitti. In the portraits of Francesco Maria della Rovere and his wife, Eleanora Gonzaga, at the Uffizi, a heroic exaltation of his subjects is evidently the intent of the artist, though even here Titian's refined color dominates the painting. The *Portrait of Pietro Aretino* in the Pitti is a perfect study of character; also in the Pitti is the so-called *Portrait of a Young Englishman,* in which the form is heightened by the use of light over color.

Titian's manner was somewhat followed by Bernardino Licinio in his *Madonna and Child with St. Francis* at the Uffizi, while Savoldo in the *Transfiguration,* also in the Uffizi, shows the particularly luminous quality of his art, not at all diminished by the inevitable influence of Venetian color in his painting. Dosso Dossi was above all impressed by the works of Giorgione and Titian; Giorgionesque is the painting in the Pitti of the *Nymph Pursued by a Satyr,* while his *John the Baptist,* also in the Pitti, is closer to Titian. His *Sorcery,* in the Uffizi, belongs to his last period, when he had created a highly personal style expressed in lush colors. Paris Bordone was also influenced by Titian, above all in his portraits, such as the *Portrait of a Woman* in the Pitti, with its powerful lines even in the architectural background, and still more in the *Man with a Fur Coat* at the Uffizi, though here the forms are more rigid and allude to the examples of other Venetians, such as Pordenone and Lotto. Bonifacio Veronese recalls Titian in his *Rest on the Flight to Egypt* at the Pitti, in the breadth of the landscape and the idyllic composition, while Giambattista Moroni is rather influenced by Moretto and Lotto in his *Portrait of a Man with a Book* at the Uffizi. He is very skillful in rendering the reality of the personages he portrays, and there is a wonderful feeling for material in the *Portrait of a Lady* in the Pitti, as well as in the *Portrait of Count Pietro Secco-Suardi* at the Uffizi. Later, in the *Portrait of Giovanni Antonio Pantera,* he does not disdain the work of Titian and Veronese; his figures always faithfully reflect the life of his time.

Another great Venetian painter of the *cinquecento*, Jacopo Tintoretto, is represented in Florence principally by the two figures of *Christ* and the *Samaritan Woman at the Well*, in the Uffizi, where traits of Michelangelo's style are enlivened by his own particular luminous construction. A notable series of portraits by Tintoretto include the *Portrait of Admiral Veniero* at the Uffizi, brilliant in the color of his coat and armor, and the *Portrait of Vincenzo Zeno*, at the Pitti, lively in its every detail. Paolo Veronese is represented by the lovely *Holy Family* in the Uffizi, highly original in composition, and by the portrait thought to be that of Daniele Barbaro at the Pitti, of a highly decorative effect. The beautiful *Annunciation* and the *Martyrdom of St. Justina* of the Uffizi, formerly attributed to Veronese, are instead, as Berenson has pointed out, by his collaborator, Giambattista Zelotti. The large number of painters influenced by Veronese is represented by Felice Brusasorci with his lovely *Bathsheba at the Bath*. Of Bassano particularly noteworthy are the *Christ in the House of Martha and Mary* and the *Martyrdom of St. Catherine* in the Pitti, in which latter painting the influence of Tintoretto is combined with the characteristic style that Francesco Bassano had inherited from his father, Jacopo.

The conspicuous examples of Florentine Mannerism are based primarily on the works of Pontormo: we have at the Uffizi the *Portrait of a Musician*, pervaded with striking contrasts of light and shadow, and the *Woman with a Basket of Spindles*, soft in forms and delicate in color; the *Leda* shows the evident influence of Leonardo's art, while in the later *Portrait of Cosimo the Elder* there is a complete harmony between color and line, each equally vivid, as in the *Madonna and Child with Two Saints*. But the *Adoration of the Magi* in the Pitti testifies more clearly the influence of Dürer, who also contributed to Pontormo's artistic education. *The Supper at Emmaus* in the Uffizi, that follows the frescoes in the Certosa di Val d'Ema, is pervaded by light which seeks out and creates the form. His forms become more ample in the *Charity*, also in the Uffizi. This is also the moment of the famous and highly original *Deposition* in the church of Santa Felicita, very similar in the quality of style to the *Portrait of a Man*, and to the *desco da parto* (a gift intended for the mother of a newly born child) of the *Birth of the Baptist*, in the Uffizi. After this circular panel, a certain decline is evident in the artist's work, as in the *Martyrdom of the Eleven Thousand* in the Pitti, or in the *St. Anthony Abbot* in the Uffizi, and still more in the *Expulsion from Paradise* in the same Gallery.

Rosso Fiorentino was inspired by Fra Bartolommeo and Andrea del Sarto in his *Madonna Enthroned* in the Uffizi, which preceded the more animated and vivid *Music-Making Putto*. A complete originality of types, in composition and color, is to be found in the *Madonna and Child with Saints* in the Pitti, and a more firm modeling in the *Moses Defending the Daughters of Jethro*, in the Uffizi. Another follower of Fra Bartolommeo is Domenico Puligo, whose *Madonna and Child with Infant St. John* is in the Pitti. He is rather closer to Andrea del Sarto in the youthful *Portrait of Pietro Carnesecchi* or in his other *Madonna* and in the *Magdalen* in the same gallery. Among the Sienese painters Beccafumi is represented in the Pitti by a *Holy Family* in which his derivation from Sodoma is evdent, while the strictest Raphaelesque tradition is visible in the *Martyrdom of St. Sebastian* at the Uffizi by Girolamo Genga, a painter from The Marches.

Agnolo Bronzino was greatly influenced by Pontormo, but he soon affirms his own personality as an excellent portrait painter, attaining a polished and refined form combined with vivid colors. In the Uffizi we have the portraits of Cosimo I in armor, and of his wife Eleonora of Toledo with her son, together with portraits of the other sons, and that of a *Young Girl with a Book*. His Mannerism is no longer derived from Pontormo in the two portraits of Lucrezia and Bartolommeo Panciatichi in the same Gallery, and an even greater freedom can be seen in the *Holy Family*, in the *Pietà*, and in the *Allegory of Happiness*, where traits from Raphael are combined with suggestions from Michelangelo in some of the figures.

Among the followers of Bronzino we must mention Alessandro Allori, whose *Sacrifice of Isaac* in the Uffizi is a painting of his maturity, and Gregorio Pagani whose two small pictures of *Susanna at the Bath* and the *Chastity of Joseph*, also in the Uffizi, are noteworthy for their lively coloring. Among these painters the most independent in following the Michelangelesque tradition was Francesco Salviati who shows, in the *Charity* in the Uffizi, how the decorative effect is the principal element of his art; in his *Patience* in the Pitti he also reveals the influence of Bronzino, while in his portraits the refined form and color is sometimes touched with the influence of the Venetian school. An austere portrait painter is also Jacopino del Conte in the *Portrait of Scarlatti* in the Pitti, but Michelangelo's influence is more evident in the *Three Fates* in the same Gallery, recently attributed to him. A faithful follower of Michelangelesque motives is Battista Franco in the *Allegory of the Battle of Montemurlo*. Still completely representative of the Florentine form is Giorgio Vasari in the *Portrait of Lorenzo the Magnificent* at the Uffizi.

In the *Nativity* by the Emilian Lelio Orsi, in the *Portrait of Bartolini-Salimbeni de' Medici*, Bishop of Pisa, by Girolamo da Carpi (Carpi is a small Emilian town near Parma and Correggio), and in the *Birth of a Child* attributed to the Parmesan Bertoia—all located in the Pitti—the tradition of Correggio and Parmigianino is naturally much stronger than that of Michelangelo. Venetian influences are noticeable in the *Portrait of a Lady* by the Bolognese Lavinia Fontana, while Giulio Campi is faithful to the Lombard-Venetian tradition in his *Portrait of a Guitar Player* and in the portrait of his father in the Uffizi. Quite different

6

TITIAN : *Venetian/1490?–1576/*PORTRAIT OF A MAN*/Canvas/56¼ x 36⅝″/Pitti*

Probably done in the years between 1540 and 1545, the painting came to Florence from Urbino in 1631. Some old catalogues of the Uffizi mention it as a portrait of Howard, Duke of Norfolk, and it has often been called a "Portrait of a Young Englishman." This identification, however, is quite arbitrary. Some suppose it to represent Guidobaldo, Duke of Urbino, and others, Ippolito Riminaldi. Still another hypothesis, and perhaps the best one, recognizes the subject as Ottavio Farnese. In this work Titian transcends the limitations of his medium to give us a figure of absolute perfection, which has even more vitality and presence than a living model. Life itself is expressed in this face, dreamy and mysterious, whose blue eyes communicate with the spectator. It is one of the finest portraits in all art, and our ignorance of the subject's identity takes nothing from our enjoyment.

from the Cremonese Campi is another Lombard of the provinces, Lattanzio Gambara from Brescia, whose *Deposition* in the Pitti reveals a strong influence of Correggio. Another painter from Brescia, Girolamo Muziano, is attracted in Rome by the style of Sebastiano del Piombo, as we can see in his *Portrait of a Gentleman* in the Uffizi. The Veronese Ligozzi, during a protracted stay in Florence, embraced the Tuscan tradition, as is evident in the *Portrait of the Grand Duke Francesco* and, with a minor breadth of form, in the *Virgin Appearing to St. Francis* and in the *Judith*, all in the Pitti.

Among the last Tuscan Mannerists, Empoli and Cigoli are worthy of note. The former is present at the Uffizi in the two lovely pictures of the *Drunkenness of Noah* and the *Sacrifice of Isaac*, in which an intense color and a strong expression are achieved, and at the Pitti with *St. Ivo*, the protector of school children, which still shows the search for a defined form of color and a contrast of light and shade, and with the two still lifes, wonderful for the sense of light that predominates in them, giving life and form to every detail. Cigoli derived his original inspiration from Alessandro Allori, as we can see in the *Madonna* and in the *Magdalen* in the Pitti; the intense color of the *Martyrdom of St. Stephen* also in the Pitti, shows the influence of Venetian painting, though in the *Sacrifice of Isaac* and in the *Ecce Homo* there is a return to more Tuscan modes of expression. This is true also of Cigoli's *Deposition*, though here his style approaches that of Baroccio; in the *Calling of St. Peter* and in the small *Supper at Emmaus*, we are aware of the influence of Correggio's work, while his *St. Francis at Prayer* is already Baroque. Andrea Boscoli is another interesting Florentine figure of this period, whose charming *Birth of the Virgin* at the Pitti is intense in color and expressed with elegance. Scipione Pulzone, the Roman portraitist, is represented at the Pitti by his *Portrait of Maria de' Medici*, inspired by Bronzino and by the Flemish school.

The close of the *cinquecento* is represented in our gallery by two painters, Federico Barocci and Annibale Carracci. Barocci attempted an eclectic combination of Mannerism and the styles of earlier *cinquecento* masters— especially of Correggio. His *Madonna del Popolo* at the Uffizi perfectly illustrates his original personality, while his *Portrait of Francesco Maria II della Rovere* and his *Portrait of a Girl*, both in the Uffizi, and the *Portrait of Federigo di Urbino* in the Pitti are beautifully decorative, with exquisitely delicate forms. The Bolognese Annibale Carracci is principally represented by his *Christ in Glory* in the Pitti, which is pervaded with a Roman solemnity.
The appearance of Caravaggio marks a revolutionary change in Italian painting. The *Bacchus* in the Uffizi, one of his earliest works, already reveals some of his essential qualities, if for nothing more than the

absolute novelty of the subject and for the unprecedented attention given to the secondary details of the composition, which are artistically expressed in their own right. Caravaggio is represented in Florence by other works, though they are not among his best. This is true also of his followers, among whom Artemisia Gentileschi is here principally noteworthy. Her *Magdalen* in the Pitti and her *Judith and Holofernes* at the Uffizi are not at all homogeneous in conception, the former being soft and gentle, while the latter overflows with energy and dramatic power.

Among the foreign painters living in Italy who belonged to that school we should mention Gherardo delle Notti (Gerard van Honthorst), with his gay *Banquet* at the Uffizi. The great decorative Baroque painting flourishing in Rome by this time had one of its notable representatives in Pietro da Cortona, who has left some of his best works in the frescoes of the Sala della Stufa in the Pitti, and in the slightly later ones in the rooms which the Grand Duke arranged as a gallery. The earlier frescoes are refined and vibrate with color, while the latter are admirable particularly for their profound conception and their perfect fusion with the plastic decoration which frames them. Ciro Ferri completed the decoration of the Hall of Saturn, left unfinished by Pietro da Cortona. The academic Carlo Maratta, in his *Vision of St. Philip Neri* in the Pitti, one of his most refined works, marks a return to the Raphaelesque tradition, but also alludes to the coming of Neo-Classicism.

In Bologna the classic and academic tendency was introduced by the Carracci. One of its most eminent representatives is Guercino, whose *Resurrection of Tabitha,* an early work in the Pitti, is strongly modeled and is rich in that luminosity which marked his later work. The Florentine painters were far less Baroque than their other Italian contemporaries. Cigoli is followed by Bilivert, who perhaps surpasses his master in the delicacy of color in his painting of the *Archangel Raphael Refusing the Gifts of Tobias,* in the Pitti. Francesco Furini, a pupil of Matteo Rosselli, painted some lovely nudes, in which the drawing is not inferior to the soft and delicate chiaroscuro; his *Ila and the Nymphs* and *Adam and Eve,* both at the Pitti, are among his best works. Cristofano Allori's *Judith* fully deserves the renown it enjoys; its delicate drawing and perfectly blended warm coloring make it the most beautiful Florentine painting of the *seicento* (seventeenth century). Volterrano should be mentioned for the pleasing painting entitled the *Jest of Vicar Arlotto.*

Other Italian schools of the *seicento* are also represented by excellent works: the Genoese Bernardo Strozzi's *Christ and the Pharisees,* painted during his Venetian period, has a cleaner color than those we find in his earlier works; Bernardo Cavallino from Naples is represented by his *Esther and Ahasuerus,* a delicate and refined work in which the composition

43

peculiar to this painter is evident. And above all there is Salvator Rosa; called to Florence by the Medici, he left here some of his best and most pleasing works: *Landscape with a Broken Bridge,* a so-called *Seascape of the Towers,* the *Wood of Philosophers,* and the *Battle,* all at the Pitti. Here we have the fantastic interpretation of reality, in which is displayed all the poetic temper of the artist who was a truly spontaneous poet.

The same may be said for Venetian *seicento* painting, which is represented by the works of Domenico Fetti: *Artemisia* at the Uffizi and the *Parable of the Lost Drachma* at the Pitti, in which the artist's complete assimilation of Venetian painting is evident. The Uffizi also owns the *Toilet of Venus* and the *Sacrifice of Isaac* by Jan Lys, who was also strongly influenced by Venetian art. In the *settecento* (eighteenth century) Venice was still a leading center of Italian painting. The two views by Canaletto at the Uffizi, the *Palazzo Ducale and the Piazzetta of San Marco* and the *Canal Grande at the Ponte di Rialto,* have a clarity and brightness which place them among the best works by the chief figure in this school. In Bologna the principal artist at this time is Giuseppe Maria Crespi, whose pleasant *Fair at Poggio a Caiano* is now at the Uffizi. But Neo-Classicism was becoming stronger; and with the mythological scenes of Pompeo Batoni we approach the first flourishing of the Neo-Classical school in Rome, of which Batoni is the first and most eminent representative.

THE PICTURE SECTION

7

CIMABUE : *Florentine/c.1240–1302/*MADONNA AND CHILD WITH SAINTS/*Panel/151⅝ x 87¾"/Uffizi*

Painted for the high altar of the church of Santa Trinita, this work remained in place until 1472, after which time it was removed to various chapels of the church and finally to its convent. The architectural character of the composition, accentuated by the massing of shadow areas, together with a greater restraint and rigidity, suggest that this is a late work, following the frescoes at Assisi begun in 1277. Vasari says that Cimabue gave "the first light to the art of painting"; and this panel, more than any other by him or his predecessors, is really a foundation work of the new Italian painting. Its monumentality is remote from strict Byzantine influence; and if we can find some precedent for this painting in the Florentine art of the thirteenth century, it still differs completely in the imprint of originality which the genius of the artist has given it. It surpasses the other *Madonna* which can be surely attributed to Cimabue, now at the Louvre.

GIOTTO : *Florentine / c. 1267–1337 /* THE MADONNA IN
MAJESTY */Panel/128 x 80¼″/Uffizi*

Painted for the Florentine church of Ognissanti
around 1310, this panel is later than the famous frescoes
of the Scrovegni chapel at Padua. Compared with Cimabue's panel, opposite, it reveals a new art, completely free
from all vestiges of Byzantine style, idealizing and en-
nobling the forms of reality. The composition, though
again representing an enthroned Madonna, takes on a
different character due to the way the figures are placed
around her, grouped so as to take part in the action, with
eyes turned toward her in silent ecstasy. But above all, it
is the figure of the Madonna which, for all the power of
its forms and the solemnity of attitude, still expresses the
new humanity of Giotto's art. This art is revealed by the
simplicity of the unpretentious dress, the natural drapery
of the mantle, the fullness of the modeling, but principally
by a feeling of sublime motherhood which comes from
her look and her way of holding the Child, who also is
full of life in his tidy clothes, and majestic in the simplicity of his act of blessing.

9 (at left)

GIOTTINO : *Florentine/active 1324–1369/*THE DEPOSI-
TION*/Panel/76¾ x 52¾″/Uffizi*

The identity of the painter of this panel is still a
subject of debate. He is mentioned by Vasari as Tommaso
di Stefano, called Giottino—a name which probably con-
fuses the work of more than one artist. Actually, he is
probably the painter Giotto di maestro Stefano, called
Giottino; and should be distinguished from two other
painters, Maso and Stefano, who are mentioned as pupils
of the great Giotto. Since the painting belonged to the
church of San Remigio, St. Remigius is represented here,
with St. Benedict and the usual persons of the scene. The
date which is most probable for this painting—the second
half of the fourteenth century—accounts for the presence
of elements of diverse origin, for it was a time of non-
Tuscan influence in Florentine painting. Despite these
elements, like certain North Italian traits, the work has a
particularly Florentine character which expresses itself in
a sobriety of composition and a balanced harmony of
attitudes, and at the same time manages to be highly
dramatic.

10 (above)

STARNINA : *Florentine/died before 1413/*THE THEBAID*/
Panel/81⅞ x 29½″/Uffizi*

Acquired by Lamberto Cristiano Gori of Florence in
1780 with an attribution to Starnina; later attributions
were to Pietro Lorenzetti, owing to certain Sienese traits;
and still later to a miniature painter such as Lorenzo
Monaco was in his youth, or at least to someone of his
school. There can be no doubt that this is the work of a
late fourteenth-century Florentine painter who had contact with numerous masters and various relationships with
such painters as Lorenzo Monaco, Masolino, and Paolo
Uccello; the last two were considered his pupils. It is very
probably a work of Starnina, who in this panel shows
how he developed the teachings of Antonio Veneziano
and Agnolo Gaddi—with the latter he had collaborated
in the Castellani chapel in Santa Croce—attaining a firm-
ness and relief in the modeling of the forms which are at
the same time imbued with something of the living quality
of nature.

11

SIMONE MARTINI : *Central Italian/1284–1344/*THE ANNUNCIATION*/Panel/104⅛ x 120⅛″/Uffizi*

     Justly one of the most famous of all Italian paintings. With its Gothic grace, its sinuous, cursive lines which create movement, with its precious color and its refined elegance, this is a superb example of the elevation of style reached by the Sienese school. The Virgin seems to be leaning gently on the throne, and the expression of her face accentuates her shyness with its sorrowful resignation. Not less idealized is the figure of the angel, graceful, lovely, and yet solemn.

12

GENTILE DA FABRIANO : *Central Italian/1360?–1427?/*THE ADORATION OF THE MAGI/*Panel/118⅛ x 111″/Uffizi*

Signed and dated 1423, this work was painted for the chapel of Palla Strozzi in the sacristy of the church of Santa Trinita in Florence, where it remained until the early nineteenth century. This large altarpiece still reflects the traits of the so-called "International Gothic," a style in which Gentile was one of the foremost masters. The fairy-tale atmosphere of the composition can hardly be surpassed, with its wealth of motifs, the comeliness of the forms, the vivacious coloring, and the feeling of pomp and sumptuousness which the panel creates. But it should be noted that, perhaps just because of contact with Florentine art, there came about that perfect unity of representation and vigor of construction which permitted the artist to create his masterpiece. The landscape and all the naturalistic bits which Gentile has crowded into his picture reveal a love of details which interests us more than the pleasure we get from merely contemplating the story, attractive as it is.

13 (at left)

AMBROGIO LORENZETTI : *Central Italian/died 1348?/*
PRESENTATION IN THE TEMPLE/*Panel/101 x 66"/Uffizi*

A late work of the master, the painting is signed
and dated 1342. It comes from the Sienese hospital of SS.
Gregory and Nicholas in Sasso, called the Hospital of
Monna Agnesa, after its founder. For this hospital or for
a small church nearby Ambrogio is said also to have
painted some frescoes, now lost. Poor preservation notwithstanding, this work shows all of the painter's essential
qualities, combining Sienese grace with a solidity of form
and a depth and spaciousness of composition which reflect
his Florentine experience. And it is for his talent as a
"noble composer and designer" that Ghiberti places
Lorenzetti before Simone Martini himself, calling him
"the very best among the Sienese painters" of his own
time.

14 (above)

UCCELLO : *Florentine/c.1396–1475/*THE BATTLE OF SAN
ROMANO/*Panel/127⅛ x 71⅝"/Uffizi*

Together with two others now in the Louvre and the
National Gallery, London, this panel was probably
painted about 1455-60 for Cosimo the Elder. They all
represent the battle which took place on June 1, 1432,
when Nicola da Tolentino and Micheletto da Cotignola
led the Florentines to victory over Bernardino della
Carnia in the pay of the Milanese Filippo Maria Visconti.
The perspective achievement of the composition has recently been restored to its original state, allowing us to
see the foreshortening of the figures and the vivid, brilliant colors which give the whole scene an air of fantasy.
The painter indulged himself in drawing the forms and
masses in a simplified, geometrical manner, coloring
them with arbitrary hues. He attains a complete fusion
of reality and fantasy through a perfect stylization, so
that this panel, and the two companion panels, comprise
one of the most original and characteristic creations of
the early Florentine Renaissance.

15

LORENZO MONACO : *Florentine/c.1370–c.1423/*THE
ADORATION OF THE MAGI/*Panel/56¾ x 69⅝″/Uffizi*

This work is not dated, but it probably belongs to
the artist's last period. In it, as in his two other works at
the Uffizi (the large *Coronation of the Virgin* and the triptych with the Madonna between saints and angels) the
artist is faithful to the monastic tradition and to his
experience as a miniature painter. The elegance of its
composition, the gaiety and sweetness of its colors make
this a delightfully decorative picture. In the colors we
may see points of contact with Fra Angelico, with whom
Lorenzo Monaco certainly collaborated. This explains
why the panel had been formerly attributed to Angelico
himself. The Annunciation, the prophets, and the Holy
Father in the upper part of the picture were added at the
end of the fifteenth century by Cosimo Rosselli, to give it
a rectangular shape more suited to the taste of the time.

16

GENTILE DA FABRIANO : *Central Italian/1360?–1427?/*
THE NATIVITY/*Panel/10¼ x 24″/Uffizi*

Of the three scenes which appear on the predella of
the *Adoration of the Magi* (plate 12), this is the most
spontaneous and the most deeply pervaded by religious
feeling. Though the setting is a representation of a landscape, attention is not distracted by elaborate costumes or
architectural display, as in the other two scenes of the
predella, the *Flight into Egypt*, and the *Purification*
(which is now in the Louvre and is replaced in the Uffizi
by a copy). Still, a love of nature is evident here which
is characteristic of Gentile. It leads him to compose an
idealized landscape which, while softened with infinite
delicacy, nevertheless reveals in its naturalistic details
what he had learned from Florentine art. The panel
which is in the Louvre went there in the days of Napoleon I; and this is a case where a true international collaboration might lead to the reintegration of a work of
art now unreasonably dismembered and divided between
different museums.

MASACCIO : *Florentine/1401–1428/*MADONNA AND CHILD WITH ST. ANNE/*Panel/68⅞ x 40½″/Uffizi*

This panel was painted for the Florentine church of Sant'Ambrogio and belongs to Masaccio's youth—which explains the resemblances to the work of Masolino da Panicale (1383?–1440). He collaborated with Masaccio on the famous frescoes in the Brancacci chapel in the church of the Carmine in Florence, and some critics believe he also collaborated on this work. But the conception of the group is doubtless Masaccio's, so that the supposed collaboration is of secondary importance. The artist already has a style of his own, formed by observing Brunelleschi and Donatello. Masaccio's talent asserts itself here on a par with those two great initiators of the Renaissance. Giotto is recalled, and also the earlier, Romanesque tradition, especially in the monumental structure of the group—which is not disturbed by a certain Gothic elegance in some of the angels. The statuesque solemnity of the figures is unmistakably Masaccio, and its equal cannot be found except in some of the creations of Piero della Francesca. The picture, damaged in a very bad restoration probably in the eighteenth century, has recently been cleaned of subsequent repaintings, and now its original majestic coherence has been recovered.

JACOPO BELLINI : *Venetian/died 1470/*THE MADONNA AND CHILD/*Panel/28¾ x 19⅝″/Uffizi*

It is perhaps to be identified with the Madonna which was in the Magistero del Monte Novissimo at Venice. The painting is interesting because it is a rare work by this artist, and also for what it reveals to us of the formation of his artistic personality. The influence of Gothic and Byzantine art is felt, along with that of his teacher, Gentile da Fabriano, and of Florentine painting. He became familiar with the latter during his stay in Florence with Gentile, and subsequently through his contacts with Paolo Uccello and Dello Delli, who came to Venice. However, Jacopo remains Venetian in his art, and attains a complete originality, here revealed in the solemn and noble placing of the figure and in the loveliness and clarity of the color. The panel, purchased in 1906, comes from the Convent of San Michele at Lucca.

19

FRA FILIPPO LIPPI : *Florentine/c. 1406–1469/*THE CORONATION OF THE VIRGIN/*Panel/78¾ x 113″/Uffizi*

Executed for Francesco d'Antonio Maringhi, chaplain of the church of Sant'Ambrogio in Florence, this work was finished in 1447 and placed on the high altar of the church. One of Filippo Lippi's most significant paintings, it clearly marks the difference between his work and that of his predecessors Masaccio and Angelico, on whom his style was formed. There is indeed in the scene a humanity which is far from Angelico's heavenly visions. Lippi's figures are taken from people around him, and show an extraordinary liveliness. A scroll adjacent to one of them bears the inscription IS PERFECIT OPUS, and this figure has been thought to be Lippi's self-portrait. However, the face seems too old for the artist, who at the time of this painting was probably about forty. The figure is now considered to be a portrait of Francesco Maringhi. The panel remained in the church until the eighteenth century. From there it passed into the hands of a dealer, who in 1813 sold it to the gallery of the Accademia, where it remained till 1919.

DOMENICO VENEZIANO : *Florentine/1390?–1461*/THE
MADONNA AND CHILD WITH SAINTS/*Panel/78¾ x 83⅞"*/
Uffizi

This signed work was painted for the high altar of
the church of Santa Lucia de' Magnoli in Florence, probably about the years 1440 and 1450. It is the artist's most
important picture, and is used in the identification of his
other works. A follower of Masaccio, he brings clear
color and daylight to Florentine painting, so that he appears as the true predecessor and master of Piero della
Francesca, who helped him in the frescoes, now lost, of
the Florentine church of Sant'Egidio. Though of Venetian origin, Domenico appears completely Florentine in
his style, and the Uffizi's panel shows him in full maturity. To a distinctive sense of coloring which sets him
apart from Florentine painters after Masaccio, he joins
a solidity of form and a power of dramatic expression
perfectly in keeping with the Florentine tradition.

21

FRA ANGELICO : *Florentine/1387?–1455/*THE CORONATION OF THE VIRGIN/*Panel/*
44⅞ x 44½"/Uffizi

     The painting belongs to the artist's early period—about 1435. It comes from
the Hospital of Santa Maria Nuova in Florence, and was probably painted for its
church, Sant'Egidio, as it is known to have been there since the fifteenth century.
Although some critics see in it the predominence of Angelico's collaborators, or even
attribute it to his school, we must accept the work as substantially by Angelico himself, due to its supreme quality and its perfect accord with the mystical vision of the
painter, as seen in other early paintings, like the *Last Judgment* in the San Marco
Museum, Florence. The background of shining gold, and the bright luminosity diffused
over the whole composition justify the title of "Paradise" often given to the picture.
It is justly one of the most famous works of the painter who, in this and in other
works, has left a testimony of his personality as an artist and a pious monk, creator
of sublime visions in exaltation of God.

22

DOMENICO GHIRLANDAIO : *Florentine/1449–1494/*THE ADORATION OF THE MAGI/ *Circular panel/Diameter 67⅜″/Uffizi*

The *tondo* bears the date 1487. It remained in the *guardaroba* of the Grand Duke of Tuscany until 1780, when it was brought to the Uffizi. Ghirlandaio's exquisitely decorative qualities are again evident in this panel, which was probably painted for the Florentine church of Orbatello. Vasari, in his life of Ghirlandaio, mentions several *tondi* by the painter, which he had seen in private homes. The painting is done in tempera, a medium preferred by the artist even though by this time there were new developments in this field. It is contemporary with the great cycle of frescoes in the apse of Santa Maria Novella. The composition attains a certain grandeur through the multitude of figures and the architectural solemnity of the background. The magnificent, multi-colored robes create a striking harmony. A workshop replica of this painting, with some variations, is in the Pitti.

23 (at left)

BALDOVINETTI : *Florentine/1425?–1499/*THE ANNUNCIA-
TION*/Panel/65¾ x 54″/Uffizi*

Executed for the church of the Salvestrian Fathers
of San Giorgio sulla Costa in Florence. Later it belonged
to the monastery of Santo Spirito and in 1868 came to the
Uffizi. It was probably painted in the year 1457, according to the most recent research of Ruth Wedgwood Ken-
nedy, who has studied this artist. It is therefore one of his
earliest works, but already announces the period of his
maturity. Though the influence of Domenico Veneziano is
evident in this painting, it cannot be denied that both
drawing and composition are peculiarly Florentine, especially in the incisive and clear outlines, and in the abun-
dance of elements which recall the surroundings and landscape familiar to the painter. The color, at times very
lively, is distributed in sober alternations among the
figures, and its heavier body reminds us of the researches
and experiences mentioned by Baldovinetti in his *Libro
di Ricordi* (Book of Records).

24 (above)

SIGNORELLI : *Central Italian/1441:4–1523/*HOLY FAM-
ILY*/Circular panel/Diameter 49″/Uffizi*

Taken from the Camera della Comunità in 1802.
According to Vasari it was painted for the audience
chamber of the Guelph chiefs in Florence, where it still
hung in 1730. The work belongs to Signorelli's bold and
strong style, and is therefore datable in the late fifteenth
century—that is, not long after the frescoes at Orvieto.
The great sculptural power of the masses foreshadows
Michelangelo, and is combined with a perfect harmony of
formal values, both in color and line, characteristic of
the maturity of the artist. The composition is rigidly laid
out according to perspective; the metallic color gives
added vigor to the forms, so organically enclosed within
the *tondo*.

25 (at left)

SIGNORELLI : *Central Italian/1441:4–1523/*THE MADON-
NA AND CHILD/*Panel/67 x 46⅛″Uffizi*

Painted for Lorenzo di Piero de' Medici, the Magnificent. From the Villa di Castello, where Vasari saw it,
the work came to the Uffizi in 1779. It was probably
painted around 1490, about the same time as the *Education of Pan* (destroyed in Berlin during the last war)
which had also been commissioned by Lorenzo. The
present work recalls the art of Piero della Francesca,
from whom Signorelli took his first inspiration; but there
are also presentiments of Michelangelo, in the almost-
nude shepherds in the landscape background, who give a
new accent to the subject without affecting its sacred
character; and in the two prophets in the monochrome
medallions in the upper corners of the picture. The fact
that Signorelli enclosed the Madonna and Child in a
circle shows us how strongly he was influenced by Florentine art immediately on coming into direct contact
with it.

26 (above)

PIERO DELLA FRANCESCA : *Central Italian/1420?–1492/*
FEDERIGO DA MONTEFELTRO, DUKE OF URBINO, AND HIS
WIFE, BATTISTA SFORZA/*Panel/18½ x 13″/Uffizi*

The two portraits were painted at Urbino in 1465–
66; according to other critics, between 1472–73, just
after the death of the Duchess. They came to Florence
with the bequest of the Della Rovere family in 1631 and
were added to the Gallery in 1773. The portraits are
admirable for the stylization of the details, and for the
original background of a distant landscape, bright and
luminous, against which the busts stand out in perfect
relief. The distinctive profile of the Duke, Federigo da
Montefeltro, expresses his personality as a leader and
patron, at once bold and prudent, generous and learned,
as he was described by his biographers. Battista Sforza,
the Duchess, appears to be more than twenty years old,
her age when Piero made this portrait, in which he lin-
gered over the details of her dress, jewels, and headdress.
Here she is more human than in the marble bust by
Francesco Laurana in the Bargello, in which she is completely idealized.

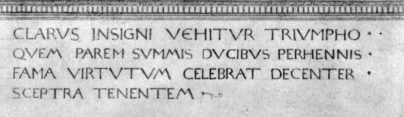

CLARVS INSIGNI VEHITVR TRIVMPHO · ·
QVEM PAREM SVMMIS DVCIBVS PERHENNIS ·
FAMA VIRTVTVM CELEBRAT DECENTER ·
SCEPTRA TENENTEM

QVEMODVM REBVS TENVIT SECVNDIS ·
CONIVGIS MAGNI DECORATA RERVM ·
LAVDE GESTARVM VOLITAT PER ORA ·
CVNCTA VIRORVM

27

PIERO DELLA FRANCESCA : *Central Italian/1420?–1492/*
ALLEGORICAL TRIUMPHS OF THE DUKE AND DUCHESS OF
URBINO/*Panel/18½ x 13″/Uffizi*

On the back of his portrait, Federigo in armor,
crowned by a Victory, is seated in a chariot drawn by
white horses and driven by an *amorino*. In front of the
Duke are seated personifications of the Cardinal Virtues.
Battista Sforza, on the back of her portrait, is also seated
in a chariot, which is drawn by two unicorns driven by
a Cupid. The Duchess holds a book; before her sit personifications of the Theological Virtues, while behind her
stand two other figures. These Triumphs follow the typical *quattrocento* classical scheme for illustrating the Triumphs of Petrarch. But Piero goes beyond the simple
ceremonious representation by giving the scenes an idealized landscape background which increases the quality of
relief and intensifies the poetic feeling. The marble para-
pet in the foreground carries a Latin inscription praising
the heroic virtues of Federigo and the feminine ones of
Battista. The perfect classical form of the lettering has the
same refinement as the painting, and gives the pictures a
final touch of solemnity.

PERUGINO : *Central Italian/c.1445:6–1523/*CHRIST IN THE GARDEN OF GETHSEMANE/*Panel/68½ x 65⅜"/Uffizi*

Painted for the Frati Ingesuati of the church of San Giusto, near Florence. When the monastery was demolished in 1529, it passed to the church of San Giovannino at the Porta Romana, and from there, in the early nineteenth century, to the Accademia. It came to the Uffizi in 1919. The painting belongs to the years between 1493 and 1497. A particular charm is given to the composition by the sunset lighting which bathes the figures of Christ and the Apostles. It is one of the most significant works of this period of the artist's activity, when he attained a means of expression all his own. Here space creates for the figures the most suitable atmosphere, obtaining both a lyrical and dramatic effect.

30 (below)

PERUGINO : *Central Italian/c. 1445:6–1532/*PORTRAIT OF FRANCESCO DELLE OPERE/*Panel/20⅛ x 17″/Uffizi*

Signed on the back and dated 1494. It came to the Uffizi from the Pitti Palace in 1833. Here, as in his other portraits, Perugino was very exact in the portrayal, and so meticulous in the execution that we are justly reminded of Flemish paintings. He has succeeded in capturing the unique character and type of the personage, who was for a long while wrongly thought to be the painter himself. An inscription on the reverse side explains clearly that it represents Francesco delle Opere (1451–1496), brother of the famous engraver of gems, Giovanni delle Corniole. The fine modeling and precision of contours, together with the vigorous bearing of the figure, make this portrait a true masterpiece, close to the other two Perugino portraits in the Uffizi of Vallombrosan monks. Though they were painted later than this portrait, they are not essentially different in quality.

29 (at left)

PERUGINO : *Central Italian/1445:6–1523/*MARY MAGDALEN/*Panel/18½ x 13⅜″/Pitti*

The remains of an old inscription on the back of this painting indicate that it was once attributed to Leonardo da Vinci. However, it is a sure work by Perugino, and one of his best, probably painted between 1496 and 1500. It represents something new and personal in the artist's career, and is far from the conventional schemes repeated in many of his paintings. It reflects more decisively the Florentine lessons he learned in Verrocchio's workshop, perhaps influenced by the example of his fellow pupil, Leonardo. As a result of this experience, the artist's habitual sentimentality was diminished, and though the result may appear at times even cold, there is a more stately grace and an intense spiritual nobility in Perugino's painting of this time. Works like this *Magdalen* show us what shaped the early art of Raphael, Perugino's most celebrated pupil.

BOTTICELLI : *Florentine/1444:5–1510/*THE BIRTH OF VE-NUS/*Canvas/68⅞ x 109⅞″/Uffizi*

The picture was painted for the villa of Castello near Florence, then owned by Lorenzo di Pier Francesco de' Medici, about the time of Botticelli's return from Rome, where he had been working on the frescoes for the Sistine Chapel. It is thus close in date to the *Primavera* (plate 2) and, like it, probably owes its inspiration to verses by Angelo Poliziano (Politian) the official poet of the Medici at that time. More clearly than any of Botticelli's other works, this painting reveals his characteristic style and his world, so remote from reality that even the pagan divinities have a kind of holy purity. Restraint governs the entire composition, so that each motion and gesture is balanced and resolved in the central figure with its pervasive melancholy. The close observation of natural phenomena, particularly notable in the sparkling wavelets, suggests the influence of Leonardo. But Botticelli's own personality is predominant in the marvelous lucidity of poetic sentiment which he attains.

BOTTICELLI : *Florentine/1444:5–1510/*PORTRAIT OF A MAN WITH A MEDAL/*Panel/22⅞ x 17⅜″/Uffizi*

The person represented has been identified by some as Pico della Mirandola, but he is more probably a member of the Medici family—either Piero "the Gouty," son of Cosimo the Elder, or his brother Giovanni. Other critics have thought the subject might be the author of the medal, who is unknown, although some without any sound basis have suggested Michelozzo. The medal itself, one of the oldest in honor of the Medici, represents Cosimo the Elder, which may indicate that the painting was executed in 1464, the year of his death. Although this is a youthful work by Botticelli, it is painted by a man already master of his craft. It has a most lively expression and is one of the most beautiful of Botticelli's portraits. Many of its details are reminiscent of Baldovinetti, whose style and whose manner of drawing, in particular, Botticelli observed closely during his early period. The landscape also recalls the style of Pollaiuolo.

PIERO DI COSIMO : *Florentine/1462–1521?/*THE IMMAC-
ULATE CONCEPTION/*Panel/81⅛ x 67¾"/Uffizi*

FILIPPINO LIPPI : *Florentine/1457–1504/*THE ADORATION
OF THE MAGI/*Panel/101⅝ x 95⅝"/Uffizi*

This painting, executed for the Tebaldi Chapel in
the church of SS. Annunziata, is described by Vasari who
remarks on how Piero has eliminated all light except that
which emanates from the dove over the Virgin's head, and
speaks of the fanciful landscape with its "singular looking trees . . . caves and grottoes." In this landscape and
in some of the details, Piero attains a highly poetic expression. The composition reveals all that original power
of imagination, direct observation of nature, and intensely
personal emotion that, together with the richly enameled
coloring, constitute the principal characteristics of his art.
The *Immaculate Conception* was acquired by Cardinal
Leopoldo de' Medici in 1670 and bequeathed to the *guardaroba* of the Medici at his death in 1675, whence in
1804 it came to the Uffizi.

The panel is inscribed on the back: FILIPPUS ME
PINSIT DE LIPIS FLORENTINUS ADDI 29 DI
MARZO 1496 (Filippo Lippi of Florence painted me on
March 29, 1496). It was painted for the church of San
Donato a Scopeto near Florence in substitution for the
one left unfinished by Leonardo (plate 46), whose influence is seen in the pyramidal structure of the composition,
and in many details. Vasari has identified many of the
personages represented. The astrologer bearing a quadrant
portrays Pier Francesco, son of the artist Lorenzo di Giovanni d'Averardo called Lorenzo di Bicci. The standing
figure of a young king with a page removing the crown
from his head is Giovanni di Pierfrancesco, father of the
condottiere Giovanni delle Bande Nere, while the young
man with long blond hair who offers him a silver chalice
is his cousin Pierfrancesco.

35

BOTTICELLI : *Florentine/1444:5–1510/*THE MADONNA ENTHRONED WITH SIX SAINTS/
Panel/133⅞ x 106¼"/Uffizi

This work, painted for the high altar of the church of San Barnaba in Florence, may probably be dated in the years after 1487 when Botticelli devoted his great activity to important secular subjects as well as to religious subjects. The monumentality of the composition is particularly notable; and the marvelously modeled figures are striking in their conception. To the right of the Madonna, the figure of the Baptist, especially, calls to mind sculpture by both Donatello and Pollaiuolo; and no less imposing is St. Catherine, at left, who is rendered with statuesque solemnity. The architectural framework in which the group is placed is likewise an imposing one. Not included in our reproduction is the incomplete predella, the little panels of which are true masterpieces due to the artist's skillful composition, narrative power, and sense of space. The painting came to the Uffizi in 1919 from the gallery of the Accademia.

36

BOTTICELLI : *Florentine/1444:5–1510/*THE ADORATION OF THE MAGI/*Panel/43¾ x 52¾"/Uffizi*

Painted about 1475 for an altar in the church of Santa Maria Novella, Florence. The composition attains its nobility through the dignified concentration of all the personages; in them the artist has portrayed the principal members of the Medici family, to whom the donor was very devoted. The king kneeling before the Christ Child has the features of Cosimo the Elder; the one robed in red, with his back to the spectator, is his son Piero "the Gouty"; and the youngest of the three is his brother Giovanni. Standing behind them is Piero's son Giuliano, and in the foreground at the left, his brother Lorenzo the Magnificent, still a very young man. The donor Giovanni del Lama appears beyond him, while at the right the artist has painted his own portrait. This altarpiece is mentioned by writers during the artist's own lifetime. In his detailed description, Vasari states: ". . . it is indeed a most admirable work . . . so beautiful that every artist who examines it is astonished . . . ."

BOTTICELLI : *Florentine/1444:5–1510/*THE CALUMNY OF APELLES*/Panel/24¾ x 36¼″/Uffizi*

This work, painted for Antonio Segni, a friend of Leonardo's, was in Vasari's day (1550) in the house of a Florentine scholar, Messer Fabio Segni. It came to the Uffizi in 1773 from the secret archives of the Pitti Palace. The *Calumny* dates from the decade 1490–1500, a period during which Botticelli was going through the religious crisis that dominated the last years of his life. Thus its pervasive sense of torment and agitation, so far from the serenity of his earlier works. This composition is a characteristic example of Renaissance thought. It was intended to reproduce a painting of Apelles desscribed by Lucian of Samosata—a theme attempted by other artists of the fifteenth and sixteenth centuries. But naturally, as was always the case in *quattrocento* Florence, the painting is really a highly personal re-creation of the artist. The jewel-like coloring, the emotional intensity of the theme, and the vibrantly dynamic composition make it a true masterpiece.

38

BOTTICELLI : *Florentine/1444:5–1510/*THE ANNUNCIA-
TION*/Panel/61⅜ x 59"/Uffizi*

Painted in 1489–90 for the Guardi Chapel in the church of Santa Maria Maddalena de' Pazzi in Florence. The panel, which came to the Uffizi in 1872, is one of the last works of the artist's mature style. It is full of profound feeling and lifelike expressiveness in the figures. It cannot, however, be attributed entirely to Botticelli, as the work of another hand is apparent in the painting. Since both composition and drawing are perfect, it seems probably that only the basic drawing was by the artist, while the actual execution was carried out by a pupil— to whom we can attribute other works—who was incapable of the limpidity and delicacy of Botticelli's coloring; he dims the light, mutes the colors, and makes the forms more ponderous.

39

MANTEGNA : *North Italian/1431–1506/*THE ASCENSION/
Panel/34 x 17"/Uffizi

Mantegna's special qualities are perhaps more obvi-
ous here than in the other two scenes of the triptych
(plates 40 and 41), especially in the marvelously fore-
shortened figure of Christ who, surrounded by a living
aureole of cherubim, stands out against a sky streaked
with clouds which only increase the immensity of the
abstract blue. The profound drama of the scene is inten-
sified by the vigor of the blessing Christ and by the attitudes of the Apostles below. Grouped around Mary, they
appeal to the Saviour with a fervor that seems almost a
desire to restrain his ascent. Here the refinement of the
landscape is appropriate to the drama: rocky precipices
in which only fragments of scant vegetation are visible
form a background for the figures of the Apostles. Achiev-
ing a maximum of power and grandeur, the artist has
infused their faces with an ever-recurring sorrow and
faith.

40

MANTEGNA : *North Italian/1431–1506/*THE CIRCUMCI-
SION*/Panel/34 x 17″/Uffizi*

The proportions of the architecture are true to Renaissance standards, but the rich decoration belongs to the
spirit of the North. Everything is precious, even the color.
The splendor of the gilded reliefs in the lunettes corresponds to the exquisite tints of the marbled walls and the
sumptuous arabesques on the pilasters. The tall, majestic
figures contribute to a scene deeply imbued with religious
feeling, in which the venerable Simeon and the austere yet
maternal Virgin command equal attention. Mantegna has
achieved this clarity and equilibrium by a technique
generally found in the miniature; but he does not stress
details and thus does not detract from the essential monumentality of the composition. The scenes in the lunettes,
representing the *Sacrifice of Isaac* and *Moses Revealing
the Tablets*, are perhaps an echo of the medieval conception which found for every episode of the Old Testament
a corresponding scene in the New, even if the particular
choice meant a departure from the traditional scheme.

41

MANTEGNA : *North Italian/1431–1506/*THE ADORATION OF THE MAGI*/Panel/30¼ x 29½"/Uffizi*

      This is the center panel of the triptych, painted about 1464 for the chapel of the Ducal Palace of the Gonzagas at Mantua. It came into the possession of Don Antonio de' Medici, who bequeathed it—divided into three parts and with this central panel attributed to Botticelli—to the Grand Duke of Tuscany in 1632. Not until 1827 were the three panels recognized as belonging to the same triptych and reunited. Painted at the beginning of Mantegna's Mantuan period, this work retains traces of the lessons learned at Padua from various Florentines—Uccello, Filippo Lippi, Castagno, and, above all, Donatello—who had brought to that region new forms and the new spirit of the Renaissance. Nevertheless Mantegna had by now achieved a very personal style, so that these influences are completely assimilated. The color especially is employed in a wholly original way, while the classical motifs are no mere archeological transcriptions but are seen afresh by the artist, and infused with life by his own temperament.

42

GIOVANNI BELLINI : *Venetian/1430?–1516/*PIETÀ*/Panel/30 x 47⅝"/Uffizi*

This painting can be dated early in the last decade of the fifteenth century. Alvise Mocenigo acquired it from the Aldobrandini Gallery in Rome for 400 ducats and gave it to the Grand Duke of Tuscany in 1798. It entered the Uffizi very soon after. Monumental in composition, the painting reveals the great power of Bellini's drawing, through which he obtains an effect of intense drama while using only tones of gray and black. The same conception is found in his *Lamentation* in the Cathedral of Toledo, but with less sublimity of expression.

43 (above)

GIOVANNI BELLINI : *Venetian/1430?–1516/*SACRED AL-
LEGORY/*Panel/28¾ x 46⅞″/Uffizi*

The work entered the Uffizi through an exchange
with the Imperial Gallery at Vienna in December 1793.
Because of its similarity in style to the San Giobbe altarpiece, this panel may be dated about 1488, that is, slightly
after the *Madonna of the Trees* in the Academy at Venice.
The subject was formerly thought to have been derived
from *The Pilgrimage of the Soul* by the fourteenth-century French poet, Guillaume de Deguilleville, but now it
is regarded as probably simply a *Sacra Conversazione*.
One requires no precise interpretation to enjoy its poetic
fantasy. The landscape, particularly, with its perfect perspective and delicate pictorial effects, seems almost an
anticipation of Giorgione. The scene takes place amid a
profound calm. The glistening splendor of the marble
surfaces is matched by the precision of the forms, the
enamel-like coloring of the figures, and the warm and
luminous atmosphere of the landscape.

44 (at right)

VERROCCHIO : *Florentine/1435–1488/*THE BAPTISM OF
CHRIST/*Panel/69⅝ x 59½″/Uffizi*

Painted about 1475 for the church of San Salvi near
Florence. It subsequently passed to the Convent of Vallombrosan nuns at Santa Verdiana and thence in 1810
to the Accademia, entering the Uffizi in 1919. The old tradition that the angel at the left was painted by Leonardo
da Vinci while he was in Verrocchio's workshop seems
acceptable; this angel differs markedly from the other
in its greater nobility and spirituality. The figure of the
Baptist with his clinging drapery and chiseled features is
in keeping with the style of Verrocchio, sculptor and goldsmith as well as painter, and contrasts with the soft modeling of the figure of Christ. The landscape, attributed by
some to Leonardo and compared with his famous landscape drawing of 1473, corresponds well with those in
other paintings by Verrocchio. There is the same treatment
of light and atmosphere which render the outlines hazy
and make the forms fade so that they appear only
sketchily in the distance.

45

LEONARDO DA VINCI : *Florentine/1452–1519/*THE AN-
NUNCIATION*/Panel/39 x 85¾″/Uffizi*

The uncertainty that formerly prevailed as to whether
this should be regarded as an authentic work of Leonardo
seems now to have been overcome, especially in view of
the identification of a drawing which is apparently related to this *Annunciation*. In fact, the observation of
nature evident in the drawing of the flowers and the
meadow, and in the angel's wings, could not be ascribed
to anyone but Leonardo. This is a youthful work, which
should probably be dated about 1472, that is, while
Leonardo was still in Verrocchio's workshop. Reminis-
cences of that master persist in the figure of the Virgin
and in the classical decoration of the marble bench; but
Leonardo's characteristic style is already evident in the
drapery, the hands, the field full of flowers, and the landscape in the distance. Some authorities doubt that the
execution was entirely by Leonardo himself; but this
seems quite unjustified, in view of the liveliness of the
coloring which may still be seen despite the alterations
of time, and the bluish light of the landscape which
makes the details so indistinct that they seem to blend
with the sky. These could be by no other hand but Leonardo's.

46

LEONARDO DA VINCI : *Florentine/1452–1519/*THE ADORATION OF THE MAGI/*Panel/*
95⅝ x 96⅞″/Uffizi

Leonardo received the commission for this work in March, 1481 from the
monks of San Donato a Scopeto, for the high altar of their church, but he never completed it. The work may nevertheless be regarded as perfect; its almost total lack of
color seems no detriment. The composition with its fantastic background and tumultuous crowding in the center is a highly original treatment of the theme of the Adoration of the Magi, and exerts the fascination of profound spirituality. Although this is
still a youthful painting, it nevertheless exhibits many of the types and elements that
may be observed in Leonardo's mature style. These types and elements are entirely
different from those customarily found in representations of this subject. One notes
especially the passionate intensity of the expressions, the emphasis on the central
group of the Virgin and Child, isolated in an envelope of light, toward which all the
figures in the throng converge in a play of light and shade that runs throughout the
entire scene, accentuating the movements and the abrupt gestures.

47 (above)

GIORGIONE : *Venetian/c.1477–1510/*THE THREE AGES OF MAN/*Panel/24⅜ x 30¼″/Pitti*

This painting has been attributed to a variety of artists: to the Lombard School, Lorenzo Lotto, Morto da Feltre, and Giovanni Bellini. Now, however, it is regarded as by Giorgione, whose characteristics and hand have frequently been recognized here. The composition is indeed Giorgionesque, and the gestures, expressions, colors, and luminous shadows may all be regarded as typically his. Though some critics have noted a certain lack of vital warmth, this may in all probability be ascribed to the poor state of preservation of the painting, whose varnishes have become so completely oxidized that they do not permit easy or successful restoration. The interpretation of the subject is likewise uncertain; the customary one is both too simple and superfluous. The painting is no less interesting as a poetic composition without a precise meaning.

48 (at right)

GIORGIONE : *Venetian/c.1477–1510/*THE TRIAL OF MOSES/*Panel/35¼ x 28¼″/Uffizi*

This painting, together with its companion piece the *Judgment of Solomon*, came to the Gallery in 1795, ascribed to Giovanni Bellini. The accepted attribution to Giorgione dates from the middle of the nineteenth century, although it is generally conceded that the execution is not entirely his. The rhythmic composition, the types of figure, the landscape, and the glowing color, particularly in the group at the left, make it impossible to regard anyone but Giorgione as the originator of the work, which probably was completed by another hand. In any case, it should be dated before 1505. The subject relates to a legend of the infant Moses who took the crown from Pharaoh's head and placed it on his own. He was forced to submit to a trial by ordeal, in which fire and gold were set before him. By choosing fire, he proved his innocence and thus saved himself from certain death.

49 (at left)

GIORGIONE : *Venetian/c. 1477–1510/*A KNIGHT OF MAL-
TA*/Canvas/31½ x 25⅜"/Uffizi*

The painting was placed in the Tribune of the Uffizi
in 1677, having come to the Gallery as part of the bequest
left two years earlier by Cardinal Leopoldo de' Medici.
Paolo del Sera had probably persuaded him to acquire it,
as a Titian, in Venice in 1654. Even today, the attribution
to Giorgione is not universally accepted, in spite of the
fact that it is corroborated by an old inscription on the
back, and that its manner of painting is identical with
that found in other works by Giorgione. This portrait
should be dated after 1508, during the last period of
Giorgione's activity. The face of the knight exemplifies
perfectly the particular ideal of beauty which the artist
always sought.

50 (above)

MICHELANGELO : *Florentine/1475–1564/*HOLY FAMILY*/
Circular panel/Diameter 47¼"/Uffizi*

Painted in 1504 for the marriage of Agnolo Doni
and Maddalena Strozzi (plates 57 and 58). It is the only
sure work on panel by Michelangelo, since the unfinished
Deposition in London is not universally recognized as
his. Taking the motive of the circular panel favored by
the Florentine painters of the *quattrocento,* Michelangelo
creates a very original structure for his central group,
architecturally compact and enlivened by a spiral movement of line. The nudes in the background foreshadow
the ceiling of the Sistine Chapel, not only in the artist's
preference for sculpturesque figures, but also in that these
nudes are an integral part of the general architecture
and the energy and movement pervading the whole composition. The color accentuates the masses, enhancing
their volumes without disrupting the architectural unity
of the whole.

51 (above)

RIDOLFO DEL GHIRLANDAIO : *Florentine/1483–1561/*
PORTRAIT OF A GOLDSMITH/*Panel/16⅞ x 12¼"/Pitti*

The painting, acquired by Paolo del Sera in 1668 for
Cardinal Leopold de' Medici, was at that time ascribed to
Leonardo. It retained this attribution until the nineteenth
century, when it was recognized as a work of Ridolfo del
Ghirlandaio, the pupil of Piero di Cosimo and Fancesco
Granacci. Adolfo Venturi reverted to the old attribution,
without, however, being able to adduce any really con-
vincing evidence. The painting, like the scenes from the
life of St. Zenobius in the Uffizi, does in fact reveal Leonardo's tutelage; but this influence does not go beyond a
tasteful and facile assimilation of elements of his style
which in no way disguise the artist's own manner and
personal characteristics. The precise drawing and the
translucent, sober coloring in this portrait are quite in
accord with a particular way of interpreting light and
aerial perspective, which may account for the old attribution to Leonardo.

52 (at right)

ANDREA DEL SARTO : *Florentine/1481–1531/*THE MA-
DONNA OF THE HARPIES/*Panel/81½ x 70⅛"/Uffizi*

The painting is signed and dated 1517, and was
executed for the high altar of the church of the nuns of
St. Francis, in Via Pentolini (now Via de' Macci), in
Florence. The name of the painting is derived from the
harpies who adorn the pedestal on which the Madonna
and Child are placed. The artist, though influenced by
the greatest painters of his time, from Fra Bartolommeo
to Raphael and Michelangelo, here gives us an original
creation, in which his exquisite color sense and his characteristic subtle shadowing, especially in the flesh tones, are
employed with the greatest skill. The whole composition
has a certain grandeur: the Madonna is rather severe and
thoughtful, like those of Michelangelo, but the artist
avoided the slavish imitation of the master — which
trapped many of his contemporaries. He remained faithful
to the more typically Florentine tradition of Piero di
Cosimo and Fra Bartolommeo.

53

ANDREA DEL SARTO : *Florentine/1481–1531/*THE DISPUTE ON THE HOLY TRINITY/
Panel/91⅜ x 76″/Pitti

    The four Saints in learned discussion are Augustine, Lawrence, Peter Martyr,
and Francis; the two kneeling, Magdalen and Sebastian. It is one of the most accomplished and profound works by this artist. A painter of rare formal perfection, Andrea
in this painting reaches a summit of intellectual expression. It is especially the color
which distinguishes this work from his others—an almost Venetian color, as Berenson
has observed. With it are certain characteristic Florentine elements, such as the classical figure of St. Sebastian, who, together with Mary Magdalen, gives a wonderful
vitality to the composition.

FRA BARTOLOMMEO : *Florentine/1474–1517/*THE DEPOSITION*/Panel/62¼ x 78⅜"/*
Pitti

      Vasari tells us that this panel, then on the high altar of the church of San Jacopo fra Fossi, was started by Fra Bartolommeo in the Florentine monastery of San Gallo, and was finished by Giuliano Bugiardini. However, Vasari's information cannot be exact, since the painting shows a unity of style which excludes the possibility of collaboration with Bugiardini. It is a work entirely by Fra Bartolommeo, and one of his finest. His personal style is revealed in this work not so much by the fact that it is no longer bound by the canons of *quattrocento* painting—for this is common in Florence toward the end of the century, under the influence of Leonardo —but principally in the rare beauty of the forms, in the exquisite expression of feeling, and in the perfection of the anatomy. Andrea del Sarto used this composition by Fra Bartolommeo for his *Deposition* of 1524, now at the Pitti.

55 (at left)

RAPHAEL : *Central Italian/1483–1520/*LA GRAVIDA (THE PREGNANT WOMAN)*/Panel/26 x 20½"/Pitti*

The attribution to Raphael of this painting of a pregnant woman, dates only from the nineteenth century, but it is now generally accepted. It is a work of the artist's Florentine period, probably about the years between 1505 and 1507, when he was clearly influenced by earlier Florentine painting, and particularly by Leonardo. One may even feel in this painting some echoes of Leonardo's *Mona Lisa*. Like Raphael's other portraits, it is a masterpiece of spiritual expression and balance. Its parts are maintained in perfect equilibrium, as one may see in the face and hands of the woman, and also in the character, already *cinquecentesque*, of the figure. The artist does not linger over details, but concentrates on drawing with breadth and simplicity, matched by that wonderful serenity which pervades all his figures.

56 (at right)

RAPHAEL : *Central Italian/1483–1520/*THE MADONNA OF THE GRAND DUKE*/Panel/33⅛ x 21⅝"/Pitti*

The painting was acquired in 1799 by Ferdinando III, Grand Duke of Tuscany, for 300 sequins, and owes its name to the love this sovereign had for it; the Grand Duke never wanted to be separated from this Madonna. Also of Raphael's Florentine period, probably about 1505, this work shows, in the diminished importance of the Umbrian elements of his early style, how much the painter had developed. The sentimentality of Perugino is replaced by a pensive grace, with which the artist managed to imbue the figures. The Virgin's face is of absolute purity, and is perhaps Raphael's most profound expression of the Madonna theme. Though the dark background in which the Madonna and Child have been so naturally placed is a reminder of the work of Leonardo, and though the colors have a tonality characteristic of the Florentine school, the artist uses these elements to create original and personal forms, pervaded with that spirituality which is the essential characteristic of Raphael's creations.

57 (at left)

RAPHAEL : *Central Italian/1483–1520/*PORTRAIT OF AG-
NOLO DONI/*Panel/24¾ x 17¾"/Pitti*

Vasari saw the portraits of Agnolo Doni and his
wife, Maddalena, in the Doni house in Florence, where
they remained until the nineteenth century. They were
acquired then by the Grand Duke Leopold II for 2,500
sequins and brought to the Pitti. Probably painted about
1506, they still show some trace of the artist's Umbrian
manner, though by now the Florentine influence is predominant, and can be traced particularly to the work of
Ghirlandaio and, above all, of Leonardo. The painting's
sober form, powerful construction, and the lively contrasts between light and shade, even in the landscape,
make it one of the most significant works of Raphael's
Florentine period. Vasari says of Agnolo Doni that he
was "averse to spending money for other things, but for
paintings or sculptures, in which he greatly delighted,
he would willingly pay, although he still did so as fru-
gally as possible."

58 (at right)

RAPHAEL : *Central Italián/1483–1520/*PORTRAIT OF MAD-
DALENA DONI/*Panel/24¾ x 17⅜"/Pitti*

In the portrait of Maddalena Doni the influence of
Leonardo is still more visible than in that of her husband.
The forms are more ample, and where in the portrait of
Agnolo Doni the individual character was particularly
evident, here the artist tends more to the expression of a
type. The figure was evidently inspired by the *Mona Lisa*,
finished a year before this portrait which probably dates
1506. But the image derived from Leonardo is handled
with originality, and not imitatively; the round face
rhythmically accords with the whole figure, and the mild
character suggested by her features is like the calm serenity of the sky, which rises over the landscape in the
background.

60 (at right)

RAPHAEL : *Central Italian/1483–1520/*LA DONNA VELATA (THE LADY WITH A VEIL)*/Canvas/33½ x 25¼″/Pitti*

This portrait, called "The Lady with a Veil," was seen by Vasari in the house of Matteo Botti, a Florentine merchant; in 1619 it was bequeathed to the Grand Duke Cosimo II. Though in the last century it was not unanimously recognized as a work by Raphael, today there is no doubt about the correctness of this attribution, whether or not it is a portrait of the so-called "Fornarina," the artist's mistress. Vasari says that Raphael painted of this lady "a most beautiful portrait, which might be supposed alive." Perhaps in no other portrait do we find such a lifelike warmth and exuberance—even in the clothes, richly colored and painted with an amazingly delicate touch. Again we have a portrait in which the subject is transfigured, and in which the artist reaches the apex of his creative ability. This can be compared with the best portraits left by Raphael in his frescoes.

59 (above)

RAPHAEL : *Central Italian/1483–1520/*THE MADONNA OF THE CHAIR*/Circular panel/ Diameter 28″/Pitti*

The painting was already in the Tribune of the Uffizi in 1589, and in the eighteenth century it was brought to the Pitti. It belongs to the artist's Roman period, painted probably in 1516, when the artist was working in the Vatican on the frescoes of the Stanza d'Eliodoro. It is perhaps the most celebrated of Raphael's Madonnas and the one which most frankly exalts maternity. At the same time it realizes a deeply human ideal of beauty which speaks directly to the heart. But its purely artistic value should not be underestimated: the figures are superbly organized in the traditional form of the circular panel; lines flow easily from the Madonna to the Child to the little St. John whose position in the group gives depth to the painting, the background of which is plain. The classical influences which Raphael assimilated in Rome inspired this rarely beautiful picture, clear and concise, without any superfluous details, and enlivened by brilliant color and brushwork of unusual freshness.

61 (at left)

RAPHAEL : *Central Italian/1483–1520*/PORTRAIT OF JULIUS II/*Panel/42⅛ x 31½″/Uffizi*

Vasari mentions this portrait and tells us that it was in the church of Santa Maria del Popolo in Rome, where we know it remained from 1513 to 1591. After being in the possession of Cardinal Sfondrati, it was acquired by the Duke of Urbino, and came to Florence with the collection left by the Della Rovere family. It was already in the Gallery in 1704. The painting is later than the fresco of the *Dispute on the Sacrament* in the Vatican, which was finished in 1511. With *La Donna Velata* in the Pitti, and the portrait of Baldassare Castiglione in the Louvre, this is one of Raphael's finest portraits of that period, at which time he felt the influence of Venetian color. The work is full of life, sharp in psychological observation, and beautiful in the rendering of forms. A copy of this portrait in the Pitti was painted, according to Vasari, by Titian.

62 (at right)

RAPHAEL : *Central Italian/1483–1520*/PORTRAIT OF POPE LEO X WITH CARDINALS GIULIO DE' MEDICI AND LUIGI DE' ROSSI/*Panel/60⅝ x 50″/Uffizi*

This portrait, mentioned by Vasari, was in the Tribune of the Uffizi in 1589. Luigi de' Rossi was appointed cardinal in 1517 and died in 1519, so the portrait must have been done in those years. It belongs to the last period of the artist's activity and is perhaps the most beautiful of all his portraits, of both the Florentine and the Roman periods. Here, Raphael has composed a group with the spontaneity of ordinary vision, yet his fidelity to nature is far from mechanical, but rather is highly intelligent and artistically selective. The composition is simple, admirable in the co-ordination of the three figures, who live a life of their own in the painting, and whose spiritual and material qualities speak eloquently to our eyes. They inspire us with that sense of the absolute, which only great works of art can give us. No traces remain of the influences in Raphael's earlier works. Here his genius has attained full maturity and originality, surpassing itself in creating these immortal figures.

63

PONTORMO : *Florentine/1494–1557/*THE SUPPER
EMMAUS/*Panel/90½ x 69″/Uffizi*

Painted in 1528, the work comes from the Cert
in Val d'Ema, near Florence, where, according to Vasa
the master had taken refuge to escape the plague
1522. The biographer rightly praises the composit
painted for the *foresteria* (guest house) of the Certosa
which Pontormo "did not in any way restrain himself,
do violence to his natural manner." Vasari thinks the p
ture very beautiful, and cites for particular praise
friars whom he himself had seen, whom Pontormo
"represented as serving at table, and could not possi
be more lifelike and animated than they are." But
only for such qualities can the painting be regarded
one of the most representative works of the artist. It
the merits that we observe in the frescoes of the clois
at the Certosa, painted in the same years: noble gestu
refinement of feeling, a felicity in the types of the figur
and a soft and harmonious coloring.

64

ALBERTINELLI : *Florentine/1474–1515/*THE VISITATION*/ Panel/91⅜ x 57½"/Uffizi*

The painting, dated 1503, was in the little church of the Congregation of the Priests of the Visitation in San Michele delle Trombe, a church which is no longer standing. In 1786 it was sent to the Academy of Fine Arts and was then brought to the Uffizi. Albertinelli was greatly influenced by Fra Bartolommeo, with whom he often collaborated. In this painting, however, the intense color, which perhaps is its most striking element, is akin to that of Piero di Cosimo, whom he came to know in the shop of Cosimo Rosselli. Piero's lively and brilliant colors impressed the artist perhaps more than his characteristic chiaroscuro. No less important in this *Visitation* are the monumental composition and sure drawing which, with its superb color, make this the masterpiece of the artist, now free from all typically *quattrocento* traits.

65 (at left)

SODOMA : *North Italian/1477–1549/*st. sebastian*/Canvas/81⅛ x 60⅝″/Pitti*

This work is a processional standard painted on both sides, made in 1525 for the Compagnia di San Sebastiano in Camollia at Siena. It was acquired in 1786 for the Uffizi, whence it passed to the Pitti in 1928. The influence of Leonardo, predominant in the first period of the artist's activity, is here still visible, especially in the imaginative landscape. In the figure of the Saint, however, we are conscious of the forms and the grace of Raphael, by whom Sodoma was inspired in his maturity. Without distorting the figure, the artist achieves an intense dramatic expression, which is heightened by the contrast of the harsh and twisted shape of the tree that balances the figure with a movement in the opposite direction.

66 (below)

SEBASTIANO DEL PIOMBO : *Venetian/c. 1485–1547/*the martyrdom of st. agatha*/Panel/50 x 70⅛″/Pitti*

The painting, signed and dated 1520, came to the Uffizi with the bequest of the Della Rovere family in 1631. Mentioned by Vasari as painted for Cardinal Rangoni, deacon of the church of St. Agatha, it is a work of the artist's Roman period, when he was especially influenced by Michelangelo. But the Venetian tradition in which Sebastiano was steeped never left him; he remains as ever a wonderful colorist. Despite a succession of varied influences in his work, he never failed to rise above them all to create his own personal style. In the nude body of the Saint there is a Roman grandeur, but the artist managed to obtain a sculptural effect in his figure without losing the freshness and spontaneity of the Venetians. The two soldiers in armor who are near the praetor are especially noteworthy for the expression of strength in their faces.

67

BECCAFUMI : *Central Italian/c.1486–1551/*HOLY FAMILY*/Circular panel/Diameter 33⅛″/Uffizi*

    From the Villa del Poggio Imperiale, this *tondo* was added to the Gallery in 1795. We do not know its original provenance, but the attribution to Beccafumi is universally accepted. The various influences which contributed to the formation of the artist are here partly visible; that of Fra Bartolommeo is particularly outstanding. Beccafumi's gift as a colorist constitutes his principal characteristic and won for him a well deserved renown: his color is especially remarkable for its luminous quality.

68

TITIAN : *Venetian/1490?–1576/*MADONNA AND CHILD WITH ST. JOHN BAPTIST AND ST. ANTHONY ABBOT/*Canvas/ 31¼ x 45½"/Uffizi*

This painting belonged to the Archduke Leopold Wilhelm of Austria; through an exchange with the Imperial Gallery of Vienna it came to the Uffizi in December 1793. In this signed, youthful work, executed about 1505, the compositional scheme was inspired by Giovanni Bellini, but Titian has radically transformed it. This is particularly noticeable in the movement—of the figures in depth and in the flowing curtains; in the sketchiness of the landscape; and especially in the sensuous use of color, which now becomes the principal element in building the forms. The types of figures in this, as in his other Holy Families of this period, have a new aspect. Particularly remarkable is the figure of St. Anthony, with his long white beard; looking like a prophet, noble and solemn, he moves toward the Madonna to take part in the action in a natural, human way. The roses offered to the Holy Child by the little St. John suggested the popular name for this painting: "The Madonna of the Roses."

69 (at left)

TITIAN : *Venetian/1490?–1576/*MARY MAGDALEN*/Panel/ 33⅛ x 27⅛"/Pitti*

This is a signed work. It came to Florence from Urbino in 1631 with the other pictures of the Della Rovere family inherited by the Grand Duchess Vittoria, wife of Ferdinando II. Vasari mentions a painting in the *guardaroba* of Francesco Maria Duke of Urbino: a "half-length of St. Mary Magdalen, with disheveled hair, which is . . . very beautiful," and Ridolfi confirms that the artist painted in Urbino "for the Duke a figure of St. Mary Magdalen in contemplation." The hypothesis that this is a replica of a lost Magdalen painted for Philip II of Spain must therefore be rejected. The work must have been executed between 1530 and 1540, when the Duke and Titian were particularly close. At this time the artist's style was mature, as the essential qualities of the painting clearly demonstrate; it is bold and spontaneous, and admirable for the vitality of flesh tones and for the richness of the Saint's golden hair.

70 (above)

TITIAN : *Venetian/1490?–1576/*PORTRAIT OF TOMMASO MOSTI*/Canvas/33⅛ x 26"/Pitti*

Tommaso Mosti, who was the secretary of Duke Alfonso d'Este, belonged to an ancient family of Ferrara, and was probably the brother of Agostino Mosti, a pupil of Ariosto. An inscription on the back of the painting, but not contemporary with it, gives its date as 1526. Some students tend to date the work a few years earlier because of the more solid construction of the figure, which reminds us of the *Concert* (plate 71), formerly attributed to Giorgione. But in this portrait Giorgione's influence has been elaborated on with greater originality than in Titian's earlier portraits. We note particularly the luminosity of color, as in the cap and in the fur-lined sleeves of Mosti's robe. Because of Mosti's relationship with the Duke of Ferrara, the portrait cannot have been painted prior to 1516, if, of course, the subject is the same person indicated in the inscription.

71 (above)

TITIAN : *Venetian/1490?–1576/*THE CONCERT*/Canvas/*
43 x 48⅜"/Pitti

Acquired in 1654 by Cardinal Leopoldo de' Medici as a work by Giorgione, and considered as such to the end of the nineteenth century, when it was recognized as a youthful work by Titian. It is certainly one of the most Giorgionesque of Titian's works, but here he adds to the poetry of Giorgione a feeling for humanity which comes from his own sense of reality. We see this particularly in the central figure, which is among the most fascinating in all Italian painting. The artist's keen psychological insight is revealed here, but especially remarkable is the suggestion of the complete oneness of the musician, and the music which his nervous hands produce on the clavichord. Even if today some do not accept the attribution to Titian, the work remains one of the most glorious masterpieces of all time—a truly incomparable artistic creation.

72 (at right)

TITIAN : *Venetian/1490?–1576/*FLORA*/Canvas/31⅛ x*
24¾"/Uffizi

In the first half of the seventeenth century the work belonged to Don Alonso Lopez, Spanish ambassador to Amsterdam. Then it belonged to the Archduke Leopold Wilhelm of Austria, and afterward to the Imperial Gallery of Vienna, whence it came to the Uffizi through an exchange in December 1793. Like the *Assumption of the Virgin* in the church of the Frari in Venice and the *Annunciation* of Treviso, it is thought to date about 1515. Some, however, consider it a later work, between 1520 and 1525. It is not a portrait, but rather the ideal type of feminine beauty as Titian conceived it: a woman ripely formed, with golden hair, and clear, rosy-tinted flesh. The perfect oval of the face, gently inclined toward the right, has something withdrawn and unreal about it, which still goes well with the luscious body, lightly covered by almost transparent material.

TITIAN : *Venetian /1490?–1576/*PORTRAIT OF FRANCESCO MARIA DELLA ROVERE/*Canvas/56¼ x 39⅜"/Uffizi*

This is a signed work, painted between 1536 and 1538. It was brought to Florence with the collection of the Della Rovere family in 1631. From the *guardaroba* of the Grand Duke it entered the Gallery in 1795. A magnificent work, says Vasari, and he mentions the sonnet composed by Pietro Aretino to celebrate it. The serious and thoughtful bearing of the Duke, who was one of the greatest military leaders of his time, is in perfect accord with the splendor of the armor and the costume, painted with such richness. Pride, boldness, and the power of a ruling spirit mark this portrait, in which Titian's color is at its most expressive. In the Uffizi there is a drawing showing the entire figure, and it was probably first conceived in this way and then reduced, perhaps to be used as a pendant to a portrait of the Duchess Eleonora.

TITIAN : *Venetian/1490?–1576/*LA BELLA/*Canvas/35 x 29½"/Pitti*

Painted about 1536–37, it probably came from Urbino in 1631 with the bequest of the Della Rovere family. The identification of *La Bella* with Eleonora Gonzaga, Duchess of Urbino and wife of Francesco Maria della Rovere, is uncertain; whoever she may be, the same person was evidently the model for the *Venus* at the Uffizi. Apart from the identity of the personage, this remains one of the most beautiful and significant portraits left by Titian, not so much for the beauty of the face, which accounts for its traditional name of *La Bella*, as for the perfect harmony which pervades the whole figure. Her luxurious dress gave the artist a chance to create a wonderful chording of colors, to accompany the flesh tones and golden hair of the subject, resplendent in jewelry and pearls. Also worthy of note is the ample presence of the three-quarter-length figure, a pattern destined to become extremely popular within a short time after the picture was painted.

VASARI : *Florentine/1511–1574/*PORTRAIT OF LORENZO THE MAGNIFICENT/*Panel/*
35⅜ x 28⅜"/Uffizi

In Vasari's time this portrait was owned by Ottaviano de' Medici, and is
first mentioned as belonging to the Uffizi in the inventory of 1784. The portrait was
executed in 1534, commissioned by the Duke Alessandro de' Medici. In fact, in a
letter written in January of that year to the Duke, Vasari describes how he intends to
represent Lorenzo. We do not know who was the model for the portrait, but in any
case it differs considerably from the contemporary likenesses of Lorenzo both in
expression and form, and cannot be considered among the more faithful representations. The artist has undoubtedly made concessions to the courtly taste and heroic
style of his time, as we know from the allegorical explanation of the details in Vasari's
letter.

76

BORDONE : *Venetian/1500–1571/*PORTRAIT OF A WOMAN/
Canvas/41¾ x 32¼″/Pitti

This work comes from the bequest of Cardinal Leopoldo de' Medici. It was traditionally called the "Nurse
of the Medici," but is instead probably the portrait of a
noble lady. Some have found it close to the portrait of *A
Lady of the Brignole Family* in the National Gallery in
London, but that work is later than the Uffizi portrait.
However, comparison with other portraits by the artist
indicates that this painting probably dates about 1530.
The influence of Titian is evident here, as in all Bordone's
works, principally in the modeling of the face and in the
way in which the color of the robe is handled. Venturi
has justly pointed out the influence of Lombard painting
in this work, which is particularly noticeable in its architectural background.

BRONZINO : *Florentine/1502–1572/*PORTRAIT OF ELEONORA OF TOLEDO WITH HER SON GIOVANNI/*Panel/45¼ x 37¾"/Uffizi*

This painting of the wife and son of Cosimo I de' Medici was in the Medici villa at Petraia, near Florence, and came to the Gallery in 1798. It must have been painted about 1550, since the boy was born in 1543 and here appears to be about seven years old. This type of courtly portrait, of Spanish gravity and rigidity, was created by Bronzino when he became, in 1540, the painter to the new Medici court under Cosimo I. The static bearing of the figures is consistent with the meticulous rendering of the picture. The twilight landscape, brightened by mirrors of water under a rich, nocturnal sky, is characteristic of this type of portrait. Because of his well-defined style, the distinction he confers upon his sitters, and his superb capacity for interpretation, he is one of the greatest portrait painters of the sixteenth century.

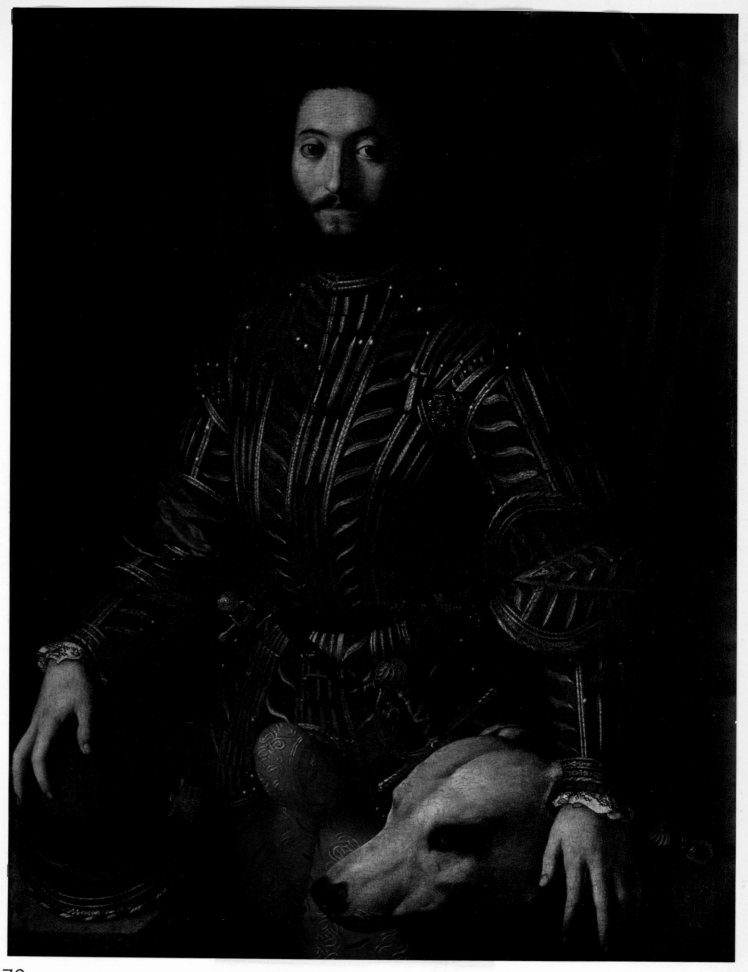

78

BRONZINO : *Florentine/1502–1572/*PORTRAIT OF GUIDOBALDO DELLA ROVERE*/Panel/*
45 x 34''/Pitti

An early work, painted when the artist was still under the influence of his
master, Pontormo. Guidobaldo had called Bronzino to decorate the Villa dell'Imperiale near Pesaro, and there he probably painted this portrait of his patron. The
work was formerly attributed to Pontormo and identified as a portrait of Ippolito
de' Medici. It came to the Uffizi from the Della Rovere bequest.

79 (at left)

SALVIATI : *Florentine / 1510–1563 /* PATIENCE */ Canvas / 69⅝ x 39¾″ / Pitti*

This work was attributed to Parmigianino when it entered the Uffizi from the bequest of Cardinal Leopoldo. It was perhaps inspired by a drawing by Vasari who mentioned it in a letter of 1551 to the Bishop of Arezzo, Bernardetto Minerbetti, who had asked to have it executed in painting for his bedroom. Vasari, in his *Ricordanze* (Records), says he himself did the painting, now lost. This one by Salviati might be a more or less faithful replica. At any rate, considering the close friendship between Salviati and Vasari, it is probable that the former had seen at least the drawing. In some parts the picture reminds us of Vasari's style, though other Florentine influences are predominant, above all that of Bronzino.

80 (at right)

SALVIATI : *Florentine/1510–1563/* CHARITY */ Panel/61⅜ x 48″ / Uffizi*

The painting came from the villa of Poggio Imperiale in 1778. Vasari mentions a *Charity* painted by Salviati for Ridolfo Landi, but Borghini in his *Riposo* cites a *Charity* in the office of the Decima. Our painting is probably this latter work, though there is some doubt as to the correct interpretation of the subject. The painting shows the essential qualities of the artist under the influence of Michelangelo, here particularly evident in the ample forms and in the spiraling movement of the composition. However, the work is not lacking in echoes of Salviati's stay in Venice during 1537–40, which resulted in a more substantial sense of color. The work must have been painted in the years between 1544 and 1548, when Salviati interrupted his Roman sojourn with a stay in Florence.

81 (at left)

PARMIGIANINO : *North Italian/1503–1540/*THE MADON-NA OF ST. ZACHARIAH*/Panel/28¾ x 23⅝″/Uffizi*

In 1605 the painting was already in the Tribune of the Uffizi. It may be one of the numerous pictures which, according to Vasari, Parmigianino painted in Rome between 1523 and 1527, and which afterward remained in the hands of Cardinal Ippolito de' Medici. The presence of certain Raphaelesque traits helps to date this work. Later on, such traits diminish as Parmigianino's artistic personality expresses itself in that original type of Mannerism of which the *Madonna with the Long Neck* is a supreme example. However, in this early Madonna there is already an elegance of line, as we may see in the shapes and the nervous drawing of the figure and the landscape.

82 (at right)

PARMIGIANINO : *North Italian/1503–1540/*THE MADON-NA WITH THE LONG NECK*/Panel/85 x 52″/Uffizi*

Vasari writes that this picture—equally famous under its Italian title, *Madonna dal Collo Lungo*—was left unfinished, and the inscription on a step of the colonnade also testifies to this. It was commissioned in 1534 by Elena Baiardi, wife of Francesco Tagliaferri of Parma, and was in their chapel in the church of Santa Maria de' Servi in Parma from 1548. In 1698 it was acquired by Prince Ferdinando de' Medici. The principal reason for the general admiration of this work is the refined beauty of its formal elements, but it is not without human warmth, for example in the heads of the children, with their animated grace that reminds one of Correggio. The artist's search for elegance, especially in the disciplined molding of the figures, allows him to obtain uncommonly exquisite effects, for which he is justly considered the greatest of the last artists of the Renaissance in Northern Italy.

83 (at left)

ROSSO FIORENTINO : *Florentine/1494–1541/*MOSES DEFENDING THE DAUGHTERS OF JETHRO*/Canvas/63 x 46⅛″/ Uffizi*

From the collection left by Don Antonio de' Medici in 1632. Vasari says that the artist painted for Giovanni Bandini "a picture of Moses slaying the Egyptian, the nude figures of this work exhibit extraordinary beauty, and there are besides many other particulars therein which are highly worthy of commendation." ("Now the priest of Midian had seven daughters: and they came and drew water, and filled the troughs to water their father's flock. And the shepherds came and drove them away: but Moses stood up and helped them, and watered their flock." Exod. 2:16-17.) The style shows the influence of Raphael and of classical sculpture, and a striking modernity of color in the strong contrasts of tints and the emphasis on the planes of light. Rosso shows here his break with the Florentine tradition, basing his art on a completely new sense of color, which distinguishes him from the other Tuscan Mannerists of the *cinquecento*. Later he played a part in the French Renaissance.

84 (below)

DOSSO DOSSI : *North Italian/c. 1479–1542/*NYMPH PURSUED BY A SATYR*/Canvas/22½ x 21″/Pitti*

The painting came from the bequest of Cardinal Leopoldo de' Medici as a work by Schiavone. Later it was attributed to Giorgione (there are elements in the painting, besides the subject, which remind one of Giorgione) or to a follower of Titian. The attribution to Dossi is due to Giovanni Morelli, who first defined for us the identity of this Ferrarese artist. The painting belongs to Dosso's youth, and it reveals the influence of Titian. The most original element of Dosso's art is his luscious color, derived, it would seem, from a fusion of the Ferrarese tradition with the example of Venice. The composition with half-length figures, the face of the nymph, and the deep tones recall the manner of Giorgione, which probably reached Dosso through Titian during the first stay in Venice.

85

CORREGGIO : *North Italian/1494–1534/*REST ON THE FLIGHT TO EGYPT/*Canvas/
43⅜ x 41¾"/Uffizi*

        Painted about 1520 for the Munari chapel in the church of San Francesco
at Correggio, the canvas was transferred in 1630 to the Ducal Galley at Modena, and
in 1649 was brought to Florence in exchange for the *Sacrifice of Isaac* by Andrea del
Sarto. A youthful work, its originality lies principally in the diagonal scheme of the
composition, and in the wooded background which encloses the scene—an altogether
new artistic device. The poses of the figures are arranged to obtain a perfect harmony
of line and mass; the drapery is designed with a sure hand, the softness of the modeling is achieved through skillful use of color, which has been brought back to its
original fullness by an expert restoration carried out twenty years ago.

CORREGGIO : *North Italian/1494–1534/*THE ADORATION OF THE CHILD/*Canvas/32 x 26⅜″/Uffizi*

Given by the Duke of Mantua to the Grand Duke Cosimo II de' Medici, the painting was brought to the Gallery in 1617. It is a work of the artist's full maturity, dating about 1522–24. Its charm, however, is somewhat contrived, no longer of solemn simplicity as in earlier representations of the same subject. The light which emanates from the Christ Child is the principal element of the picture. It bathes the figure of the Virgin, making her dress stand out sharply against the ruined temple before a luminous landscape. The profound expression of motherhood, vividly conveyed in the attitude of the Virgin, is a major reason for the great popularity of this painting.

87

CARAVAGGIO : *North Italian/1573–1610/*MEDUSA/*Circular panel/Diameter 22″/Uffizi*

According to Giovanni Baglione in his *Le vite de' pittori* (Lives of the Painters, 1642), Caravaggio did this head of Medusa on a tournament shield for Cardinal Francesco Maria del Monte. Cardinal Anton Maria del Monte presented it to Cosimo II, Grand Duke of Tuscany, in 1608, on the occasion of his marriage to Maria Maddalena of Austria. For a while the painting was preserved in the Ducal Armory. Though an early work, it must have quickly become famous, since it was the subject of two poetical compositions of the early seventeenth century, one by Gaspare Murtola, whose *Rime* were published in 1604, and the other by Giovan Battista Marino in his *Galleria*, published 1635.

ANNIBALE CARRACCI : *North Italian/1560–1609/*A BAC-
CHANTE*/Canvas/*44⅛ *x 56″/Uffizi*

This work was executed in Bologna between 1589 and
1595 for the Bolognetti family. In 1620 it was acquired
from Camillo Bolognetti for 200 ducats by the Grand
Duke Cosimo II. Cesare Malvasia, the seventeenth-century
historian of Bolognese painting, relates a tradition according to which the model for this figure of a satyr was
Annibale's cousin, Lodovico Carracci, also a famous
painter, who had interested Annibale in art. Though influenced by Correggio, Veronese, and the Bassani (Jacopo, Francesco, and Leandro) Annibale nevertheless
created his own personal style. Our *Bacchante* precedes
the artist's Roman period, and stands out, on a par with
his other works of those years, for the harmony of its
composition and for its handling of space, which gives
the painting a feeling of classical measure.

89

CARAVAGGIO : *North Italian/1573–1610/*YOUNG BACCHUS*/Canvas/38⅝ x 33½"/ Uffizi*

This painting was brought from the storeroom of the Uffizi in 1925. It is now unanimously identified as the one cited by Baglione, ". . . a Bacchus with bunches of various kinds of grapes, done with great care, but a little dry." One of the earliest, if not the very first, of the known paintings by Caravaggio—and one of his finest—it was executed in Rome between 1588–89. The fruit is painted with surprising exactness; its brilliant enameled color is not inferior to that of his greatest works. The originality and modernity of this painting strike us immediately, even before we savor the elements of the painting separately—such as the meticulous attention to the forms, the novel and bold juxtapositions of color in the figure, and the fascinating tones of the still life.

90

CARAVAGGIO : *North Italian/1573–1610/*SLEEPING CU-
PID/*Canvas/30¾ x 41⅜″/Pitti*

On the reverse side of this painting is the name of
the artist and the inscription: "in Malta 1608." The attribution to Caravaggio appears in old inventories of the
Gallery, and is generally accepted today; we know that
he was in Malta, in 1607 and 1608. In this work Caravaggio's style is fully developed. We can see this in the
strong contrasts of light and shadow, which accentuate
the essential volumes; the boy's features are intentionally
commonplace, and therefore altogether anti-classical;
and the composition is a natural and harmonious treatment of the child's body. Every non-essential detail has
been driven out by the violent lights and darks, so that
the forms acquire a new value in their exemplary simplicity and conciseness. The painting came to the Pitti
from the bequest of Cardinal Leopoldo de' Medici.

91 (at left)

BAROCCIO : *Central Italian/1535–1612/*THE MADON[NA]
DEL POPOLO/*Panel/141⅜ x 99¼"/Uffizi*

Painted for the chapel of the Fraternità dei Laici [in]
the parish church at Arezzo between 1575 and 1579 a[nd]
signed by the artist, the work was acquired in 1786 [by]
Grand Duke Pietro Leopoldo. The poise of its compo[si]-
tion, the nobility of attitudes, and the harmony of colo[r]
account for the enthusiastic admiration of the artis[t's]
contempories for this painting. Though the soft modeli[ng]
and delicate shading of the figures derive above all fro[m]
Correggio, the personal mark of the artist is nonethele[ss]
evident, especially in his distinctive conception of col[or]
for which he is considered one of the last representativ[es]
of *cinquecento* painting.

92 (at right)

VERONESE : *Venetian/1520–1588/*THE BAPTISM O[F]
CHRIST/*Canvas/77⅛ x 52⅜"/Pitti*

According to Venturi this work is contemporar[y]
with the artist's *Rape of Europa* in the Ducal Palace i[n]
Venice. It has subsequently been more precisely date[d]
about 1576 or 1577, close to the decoration of the Sal[a]
del Collegio of the same palace. The trees standing ou[t]
against the sky give a new depth to the painting; th[e]
composition is animated by contrasts of color in th[e]
figures which are conceived with grandeur and painte[d]
with broad strokes. A cryptic label on the reverse side o[f]
the painting says that it was once in a certain *scuola de[i]
Fiorentini*, not better identified. The work came to th[e]
Uffizi from Ancona in 1668.

93

VERONESE : *Venetian/1528–1588/*PORTRAIT OF DANIELE BARBARO/*Canvas/55⅛ x 42⅛"/Pitti*

Traditionally considered a portrait of Daniele Barbaro (1513–1570), ambassador of the Venetian Republic to Edward VI of England, translator of Vitruvius, and the author of a handbook on perspective. However, another portrait of this humanist in The Netherlands negates the traditional identification. Painted between 1562 and 1570, it is one of the most noble portraits by Veronese; the composition is richly satisfying, and the face is rendered with an exceptional sensibility.

RENI : *North Italian/1575–1642/*CLEOPATRA*/Canvas/48 x 37¾″/Pitti*

A late work, probably done about 1639, this painting is among those which illustrate most clearly the final evolution of Reni's art. We note particularly the refined touch, the transparent colors, and the classical simplification of the forms, all of which help redress that certain theatricality and melodrama inherent in the subject of Cleopatra's suicide. Jacob Burckhardt has remarked on the unusual sensual quality of Reni's painting of Cleopatra's hands. The picture probably came to the Gallery from the bequest of Cardinal Leopoldo de' Medici, who obtained it from the Marchese Coppi in 1640. There is a replica of the work in Madrid.

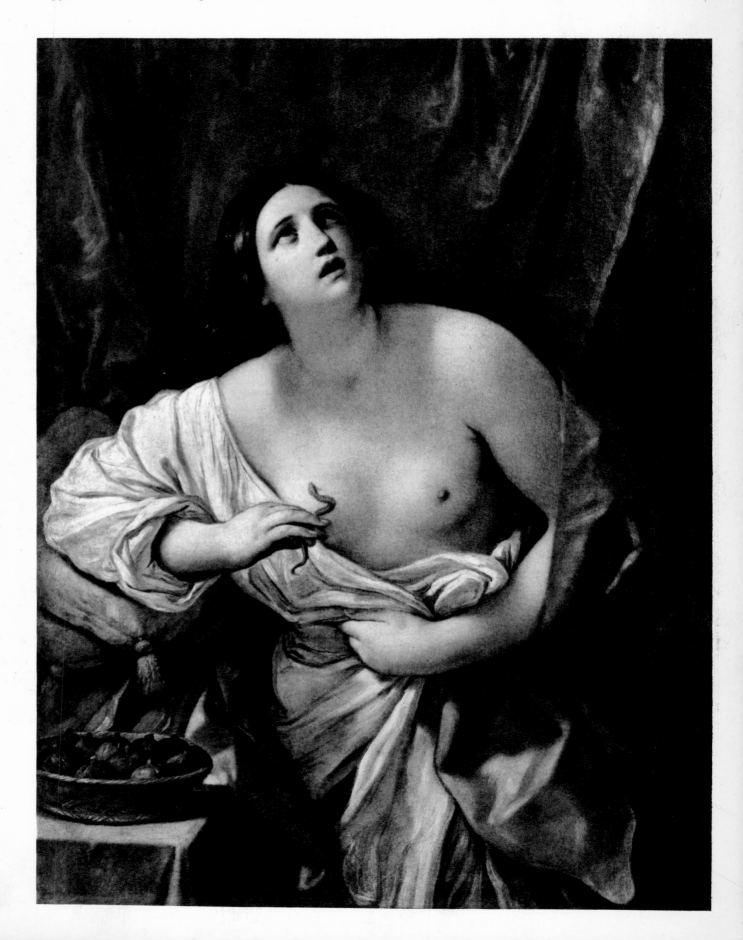

95

TINTORETTO : *Venetian/1518–1594/*PORTRAIT OF VINCENZO ZENO*/Canvas/43¼ x 34″/Pitti*

Although we know that this is a portrait of a man named Vincenzo Zeno, we do not know who he was. What we have here is another of those wonderful old Venetian noblemen whose vigorous features Tintoretto has so effectively handed down to us. The painter goes far beyond mere representation in revealing the subject's character.

TINTORETTO : *Venetian/1518–1594/*PORTRAIT OF JACOPO SANSOVINO*/Canvas/27⅝ x 25⅝"/Uffizi*

This portrait of the sculptor Jacopo Sansovino (1486–1570) was painted between 1560 and 1570. Because of the vivid characterization and the total absence of decorative details, this is one of the most interesting portraits the artist has left us. The face and hands give an extraordinary life to the composition; Tintoretto does not attempt to make a slavish imitation of his subject, but instead treats it according to his own highly personal vision. The sculptor's robe and the background of the painting are uniform, without the play of light of which Tintoretto later became so fond.

97 (at left)

TIEPOLO : *Venetian/1696–1770/*THE ERECTION OF A STATUE TO AN EMPEROR*/Canvas/165⅜ x 69¼"/Uffizi*

This work was acquired in 1900 from the Archepiscopal Seminary at Udine. It was probably part of the decoration of the palace of the Dolfin family, later seat of the seminary, which Tiepolo frescoed between 1720–25. Our canvas, though, seems a bit later than the frescoes, and was probably done about 1730. In any case, it is a youthful work, in which the painter felt the influence of Sebastiano Ricci, especially in the foreshortening of the figure of Fame, flying in the luminous sky, and in the silvery tonality of the picture, which later becomes an essential element in Tiepolo's painting. Nonetheless, the artist is here in complete command of his means of expression—in composition, in the prodigious feats of foreshortening, and finally, in the perfect chromatic harmony of the whole.

98 (at right)

MURILLO : *Spanish/1617–1682/*THE MADONNA AND CHILD*/Canvas/61¾ x 42⅛"/Pitti*

Murillo, influenced by Italian painting—though indirectly, through Rubens and Van Dyck—in this work obtains an airy and transparent effect without equal in his time. The grace and charm of the Madonna and Child explain the popularity which this painting has always enjoyed, though today we esteem some of his earlier works much more highly. The artist imparts to his Madonnas not so much a religious expression as the feeling of maternity in its most natural and spontaneous form. The work was executed probably between 1650 and 1660.

CRISTOFANI ALLORI : *Florentine/1577–1621/*JUDITH/
Canvas/54¾ x 45⅝″/Pitti

Filippo Baldinucci, a seventeenth-century chronicler
of Florentine painters, says that the painter portrayed in
Judith his own mistress Mazzafirra, in the old woman,
her mother, and in Holofernes, himself. It is painted
with Allori's habitual finish: we note the perfect composition; the form, strictly based on the painters of the
cinquecento, but still reflecting the modes of the *seicento*;
and the color and handling of tones. The pose of Judith
does not lack energy and grandeur; but a really fresh
note is struck in the treatment of the head of the old
woman and in the cushion below on the left. This picture,
done for Cardinal Allessandro Orsini, is perhaps the finest
Florentine painting of the seventeenth century, and was
celebrated by Cavalier Marino in a famous epigram in
his *Galleria*.

MAGNASCO : *North Italian/c. 1667–1747/*THE GYPSIES'
MEAL/*Canvas/22 x 28″/Uffizi*

The liveliness of composition and the boldness of
brushwork place this painting in the last years of the
artist's Tuscan period, that is, in the first decade of the
eighteenth century. His other, similar scenes of gypsy life,
some of which are still in Florentine collections, are
usually dated in this period when, as some students have
justly supposed, Magnasco was influenced by the works
of Callot and of Stefano della Bella in Florence. Magnasco was painter to the court of the Grand Duke of
Tuscany, Cosimo II, and it is said that he was married
in Florence.

VAN DER WEYDEN : *Flemish/1400–1464/*THE ENTOMBMENT*/Panel/43¼ x 37¾"/*
Uffizi

When this work came to the Gallery in 1666 from the collection left by
Cardinal Carlo de' Medici it was attributed to Dürer. There can be little doubt that
the work was painted after Van der Weyden's trip to Italy during the Holy Year of
1450. We can see this in the greater monumentality of the figures when compared with
those of his earlier works; and, as has been noted, in the placing of these figures
around Christ, who maintains the posture of the Crucifixion. This placement is exceptional in the Flemish school of that time, but not in the Italian. The high quality of
the work, altogether worthy of Van der Weyden's name, is noticeable in the structure
of the principal group and in the vigorous treatment of the figure of Mary Magdalen.

102

VAN DER GOES : *Flemish/c. 1440–1482/*THE ADORATION
OF THE SHEPHERDS/*Panel/99⅝ x 119⅝″/Uffizi*

    This alterpiece, the artist's chief masterpiece, was
painted at Ghent about 1473–75 for Tommaso Portinari,
the Medici's banking agent at Bruges. Shortly after 1490
it was sent to Florence and placed on the high altar of the
church of Sant'Egidio, where it exerted an important
influence on the Florentine painters of the time, whose
guild held their meetings in that church. The profound
religious sentiment is apparent not only in the central
scene but also in the *Annunciation* on the exterior of the
wings. The artist's extraordinary power of portraiture is
evident in the figures of the donor and his family, and in
the shepherds, whose faces are radiant with joy. No less
remarkable is the painting of the landscape and of the
flowers in the apothecary jar and glass vase in the foreground. The altarpiece was brought to the Uffizi in 1900.

103 (at left)

HONTHORST : *Dutch/1590–1656/*THE ADORATION OF TH
SHEPHERDS/*51½ x 37¾″/Uffizi*

This painting, which came to the Gallery in 179
from the villa of Poggio Imperiale, was executed in Rom
in 1621 while Honthorst was working there for the Gran
Duke of Tuscany. The work immediately attracted grea
renown and was regarded as highly unusual by the artist
contemporaries, who particularly mentioned the light tha
emanates from the Infant Christ and illuminates all th
other figures. Here one sees in the painter's work th
persistence of Caravaggio's influence, which affected hir
as soon as he settled in Rome after 1610. In that cit
Honthorst received numerous commissions for altarpiece
many of which still exist in their original sites. He als
attained great success through his secular composition
an example of which is in the Uffizi.

104 (at right)

REMBRANDT : *Dutch/1606–1669/*SELF-PORTRAIT/*Car
vas/34⅝ x 24″/Uffizi*

First mentioned in the inventory of the Uffizi Galler
in 1704, this painting was part of the bequest of Cardina
Leopoldo de' Medici (died 1675) who had acquired it i
Holland. Since Rembrandt appears here well advanced i
years, the portrait may be dated about 1664 and mu
have been purchased shortly thereafter. The representa
tion clearly reveals the destitute and pitiful condition t
which the artist had been reduced as a result of h
serious financial reverses; at the same time, like othe
works of that period, it is a testimony to the fact tha
Rembrandt's creative power was never diminished by h
misfortunes. Another self-portrait in the Uffizi shows th
artist as a young man, although his reputation was b
then already firmly established.

105

RUBENS : *Flemish/1577–1640/*PORTRAIT OF JUSTUS LIPSIUS AND HIS PUPILS*/Panel/*
64⅝ x 54¾"/Pitti

This painting, often called "The Four Philosophers," should probably be
dated about 1612–14, when Rubens was at the height of his powers. All the principal
elements of the artist's style appear fully developed here: his tremendously facile
execution, chromatic light effects, and marvelous freshness. These merits serve in great
measure to compensate for the shallowness of the psychological interpretation, a
characteristic of all Rubens' portraits, in which he tended to a somewhat superficial
rendering of his subjects' personalities.

RUBENS : *Flemish/1577–1640*/PEASANTS RETURNING FROM THE FIELDS/*Panel/47⅝ x 76⅜"/Pitti*

The painting, which formed part of the collection of the Duc de Richelieu, may be dated about 1637, that is, in the last period of Rubens' activity. The town in the background is Malines. According to the art historian Max Rooses, the landscape may be the work of an assistant, retouched and completed by the master. Rubens himself is certainly responsible for the painting of the figures and the manner in which the light plays over the scene. In any case, the work is remarkable for its grandeur. It is of the same period as the scenes from Ovid's *Metamorphoses* in the Prado and resembles them in its joyful rendering of nature.

.X.̊ IVLII. ANNO.   ETATIS ·SVÆ
.H. VIII. XXVIII.   ANNO XXXIII.

108 (below)

SUSTERMANS : *Flemish/1597–1681/*PORTRAIT OF PRINCE
CHRISTIAN OF DENMARK/*Canvas/27⅝ x 21¼″/Pitti*

The son of Frederick III of Denmark was born in
1646, and as he appears to be about sixteen or eighteen
years old in this portrait, it was probably painted about
1662. This is one of the most famous of the artist's portraits, principally owing to the thoughtful expression on
the face of the youth, which contrasts with his luxurious
garments and armor, rendered with such meticulous ac-
curacy. Sustermans, who was almost exclusively a portraitist, was official painter to the Medici court from
Cosimo II to Cosimo III. He remained faithful to Flemish
traditions and always strove to obtain the most exact
likenesses of his subjects. Although in his early work
influenced by Pourbus the Younger and Van Dyck, he
achieved a very personal style. He was active principally
in Florence, absenting himself from that city for brief
periods only.

107 (at left)

HOLBEIN, THE YOUNGER : *German/1497–1543/*POR-
TRAIT OF SIR RICHARD SOUTHWELL/*Panel/18⅝ x 15″/*
Uffizi

This portrait of Sir Richard Southwell, Privy Coun-
sellor of King Henry VIII of England, was painted in
1536. It was presented to Cosimo de' Medici in 1621 by
Thomas Howard, Earl of Arundel, to whom the Grand
Duke had expressed his desire to have a work by the
famous portraitist of Henry VIII. The portrait was placed
in the Tribune of the Uffizi with other masterpieces and
was seen there by Filippo Baldinucci who describes it in
detail in his *Notizie dei Professori del Disegno* (Accounts
of Professors of Design, 1681 ff.). This is one of the best
examples of Holbein's portrait painting, the genre in
which he excelled. It clearly reveals the artist's characteristic assimilation of Renaissance principles and his
perfect mastery of technique.

109 (below)

RUBENS : *Flemish/1577–1640/*ALLEGORY OF WAR*/Canvas/81⅛ x 135⅞"/Pitti*

Rubens painted this for the artist Justus Sustermans, whose heirs presented it to the Grand Duke Ferdinando II. Executed in Antwerp in 1638, it is thus one of Rubens' last works. Its allegorical and moralistic intent tends to be almost overlooked, for the spectator's interest is concentrated on the tremendous rush of the figures and the wonderfully harmonious colors somewhat at the expense of the interest in the subject matter. The Thirty Years' War was raging at that time, and the theme of the painting was probably related to those events, as in fact is borne out by Rubens' own reference in a letter written to accompany the picture. This also explains why in some catalogues the painting bears the title *The Thirty Years' War*. The structure of the composition is clear, despite the tumultuous figures and the sonorous orchestration of colors.

110 (at right)

VAN DYCK : *Flemish/1599–1641/*PORTRAIT OF CARDINAL GUIDO BENTIVOGLIO*/Canvas/76¾ x 57⅞"/Pitti*

The subject of this portrait, Guido Bentivoglio, author of an important history of the war in Flanders, was the private chamberlain of Pope Clement VIII. In 1607 he became Apostolic Nuncio, first in Flanders and then in France. He was elected Cardinal in 1621 and died in 1644. This portrait, painted shortly after his elevation to Cardinal, probably belongs to Van Dyck's Roman period. One of the artist's finest works, its simplicity of conception and naturalness of execution are typical of the qualities his style acquired during his experience in Italy, but which disappeared from his later painting. Its nobility and breadth of interpretation make this one of the most characteristic seventeenth-century portraits, distinguished primarily for the sense of vitality that emanates from the figure. The painting entered the Gallery with the bequest of the great Prince Ferdinando.

ALTDORFER : *German/c. 1480–1538/*THE DEPARTURE OF ST. FLORIAN*/Panel/32 x 26⅜"/Uffizi*

This and another panel in the Uffizi depicting the *Martyrdom of St. Florian* are from a series of scenes of the life of the Saint, painted about 1520. They formed part of a polyptych which was originally either in the church of St. Florian near Linz in Austria, in the chapter house of the canons there, or in the small church of St. John near the miraculous fountain of the Saint. Three panels from this polyptych are in the Museum at Nuremberg in Germany, one in the Lobkowitz Gallery at Melnik in Czechoslovakia, and still another in a private collection. The two panels in the Uffizi, both bearing the artist's monogram, came from the collection of the Spannocchi family of Siena. On the back of the *Departure* is a *Circumcision*, painted by a later and mediocre hand.

112

CRANACH : *German/1472–1553/*ST. GEORGE/*Panel/7½ x 7⅛″/Uffizi*

Although the date 1520 appears on the horse's tail, the style is still that of Cranach's youthful period, full of enchanting grace, warm and vivid color, and intensely expressive sentiment. The donor kneeling in prayer at the left, and the coat-of-arms beside him, remain unidentified. The reverse of the panel bears a representation of the head of the Saviour in a nimbus. The painting was exhibited in the Tribune of the Uffizi as early as 1635.

113

DÜRER : *German/1471–1528/*THE ADORATION OF THE MAGI/*Panel/*37½ x 44⅞"/
Uffizi

Signed with the artist's monogram and dated 1504, the *Adoration of the Magi* was painted in Nuremberg in the interval between Dürer's first journey to Italy and his long sojourn in Venice. It represents a transitional moment in his style, when the lyrical aspects of his art prevailed over the tragic. The touching intimacy of the central group of the Virgin and Child with the old king, and the straightforward manner of narration, make this probably the most attractive of Dürer's representations of the subject. The panel was formerly believed to have been painted for the Chapel of the Castello del Buonconsiglio at Trent, among other reasons because the landscape recalls a drawing of that region by Dürer. It is now thought to have been commissioned by Frederick the Wise and to have remained in the church of Wittenberg Castle till 1603, when King Christian II presented it to the Emperor Rudolph II.